THE
NEW
FAMILY
COOKBOOK

THE NEW FAMILY COOKBOOK

RECIPES FOR NOURISHING YOURSELF AND THOSE YOU LOVE

BILL EICHNER, M.D.

CHELSEA GREEN PUBLISHING COMPANY
White River Junction, Vermont
Totnes, England

Cover design by Ann Aspell.
Designed by Dede Cummings Designs.

Printed in the United States of America.

First printing, September 2000

03 02 01 00   1 2 3 4 5

Library of Congress Cataloging-in-Publication Data
    Eichner, Bill 1944-
    The new family cookbook : recipes for nourishing yourself
    and those you love / Bill Eichner.
    p.   cm.
    Includes index.
    ISBN 1-890132-48-9 (alk. paper)
    1. Cookery, America. I. Title.

TX715.E335 2000
841.5973—dc21   00-059605

Chelsea Green Publishing Company
P.O. Box 428
White River Junction, VT 05001
(800) 639-4099
www.chelseagreen.com

♥ for SARA & BERIT,
now very much on your own

CONTENTS

YOU'RE PROBABLY WONDERING
WHAT THOSE HEARTS MEAN?

  ♥♥♥   Totally healthy, you should live to 100!

   ♥♥   Don't worry if you always eat this wisely

    ♥   At least you're starting to pay attention . . .

NO HEART? Enjoy it, but not too often!

ACKNOWLEDGMENTS

A big thank-you to the professionals who helped a nonwriter get a book into print: Molly O'Neill, Ina Stern, Susan Bergholz, Elisabeth Scharlatt. Your wisdom allowed me to transform a manual of family recipes into a cookbook.

Kim Krans, Kathy Dugan, Kevin Peckham, for your hours and hours of typing.

To the generous staff at Chelsea Green, for turning several drafts of manuscripts into a book. Especially Ben Watson—your enthusiasm is contagious.

To Sonja Olson, mother of my daughters, who set a standard of excellence in the kitchen.

To Tita Jensen, sister-in-law and chef, and to other family and friends who generously shared their recipes with this eager learner.

To my ever-loving and nurturing parents, who inspired a love for food—growing it, cooking it, and eating it.

And I'm grateful to my compañera. Julia came forth with the idea that a black ring binder could become a cookbook, and then guided my hand until it was done.

HOW I LEARNED TO COOK

by Julia Alvarez

M Y HUSBAND TAUGHT ME how to cook. I know this is not a statement women usually make. Traditionally assigned the household arts, more often than not we have been the ones to introduce sons, husbands, and brothers to the mysteries of the mixer or to initiate them into the coven of the Cuisinart.

But this was not my case.

I grew up among *tías, cocineras,* and a *mami* who spent most of the day preparing the meals of that day. In the Dominican Republic of my childhood, where households were large and the extended family shared meals, cooking was no small matter.

The process began with a daily visit to the open-air market or to *el supermercado* to get fresh products. Shortages of electricity were common and refrigeration was not reliable. The meat was bought fresh—in some cases you could hear your supper bawling in the slaughterhouse behind the counter; the red snapper had been caught that very morning; the *verduras* picked just as the sun was coming up; the plantains brought in from the *conucos* of *campesinos,* their stalks still wet with sap. Often to collect all these products, Mami and the *tías* had to make many stops: to los Chinitos to get the lettuce, to Mercado Modelo for *víveres,* to *la carnicería* for meat, to Wimpy's for anything store-bought.

Once at home, the preparation began for the big noon meal. Of course, Cook had already put her *habichuelas* at slow simmer on the back of the stove. She had already cleaned the rice on a flat wooden tray and foretold my future from the fall of husks on the floor. When Mami and the *tías* arrived with their purchases, the kitchen went into high gear. The room filled with women. One *tía* rolled out dough for *pastelitos;* another mixed the ingredients of the stuffing; a third beat the eggs for the flan or seasoned the flank steak or washed the vegetables and prepared them, creating rosettes out of radishes or out of the swirled peels of carrots.

Make no mistake about it. Those women might as well have been in Michelangelo's studio: they were creating works of art, and the last thing they needed was a curious little girl underfoot. Especially one like me, whose idea of cooking was holding an orange peel above my mouth and pretending I was an English pirate raiding the Island.

"Go do something useful with yourself," Mami ordered.

"Like what?"

"Like do your homework or read a good book!"

I took my mother's advice. By the time we were settled in this country, I was a confirmed bookworm. I read and read and read. I earned scholarships and went away to school. Meanwhile, I had passed on from the cooking of my aunts and my mother to institutional cooking in boarding school and college. By the time I was old enough to be on my own in the kitchen, I did not have the slightest idea how to prepare something for myself. Everything I ate came from takeout or boxes, packages, cans. I had taken the admonition of my aunts and my mother literally; I wouldn't think of wasting time in the kitchen. I had to do something *useful* with myself, like read books.

When I met my husband ten years ago, it was in the grocery store of my new hometown. He remembers that I was carting a big plastic bottle of Sprite or Coke in my basket. He was buying buttermilk. (What the heck was buttermilk? I wondered.) He was making sourdough pancakes for breakfast for his daughters. "I see," I said. I admit I was impressed. A man who knew how to make pancakes! A man who cooked breakfast for his daughters! A man who had been to the Dominican Republic to do volunteer surgery!

His parting words were, "How about dinner sometime?"

After a childhood of being shooed out of the kitchen, I was being invited back in. My husband's idea of a date was to ask me over to his condo and cook something for me. "What would you like to eat?"

he'd ask. I knew better than to say Swiss cheese on Wheat Thins. Oh anything, I would say. He already knew I was a vegetarian. His oldest daughter Sara was also a vegetarian, so he was not one of those diehard cooks who pale at the thought of a meatless meal. I would walk into that condo and be transported back to childhood: the smell of onions frying, garlic minced and ready to throw in the stir-fry, fresh baked bread, rice steaming in a kettle.

"How do you do it?" I kept asking.

"It's easy," he kept telling me.

When we married and joined our lives together, we fell into a pattern. I did the shopping and Bill cooked. But somehow, over time, it didn't seem fair that I not contribute to our daily meal. After all, I didn't have to make a half dozen stops—to the *carnicería,* the Chinitos, the open-air market—to get the ingredients of our meal together. So, I insisted. I had to learn how to cook.

My husband would walk me through a recipe. But of course, he was so fast and efficient that I would catch myself daydreaming and drift back only to hear, "And then, when it's all ready, you put it in the oven . . ."

"Okay," I'd say, feeling too sheepish to let on that I hadn't been paying attention. So, of course, when the time came, and I found myself alone in the kitchen with two pounds of potatoes, Gruyère cheese, heavy cream, buttermilk, onions, and a mandoline, I panicked. You might as well have locked me in the cockpit of a 747 and ordered me to fly it to Paris as ask me to make Potatoes Dauphinoise out of this pile of ingredients.

But, thank goodness, my husband had written his recipes down and collected them in a small black ring binder. It was from that ring binder that I learned my first recipes: Potatoes Dauphinoise, Rhubarb Crisp, and Date Chocolate-Chip Cake. Originally, these black ring binder recipes were meager notes my husband had written for himself, but now that he was sharing his "cookbook," he had to redo the recipes in order to make the steps absolutely clear to me. I wanted straightforward instructions without the "cooking jargon" that could make me feel as if I were being asked to learn a foreign language, not just make a crème brûlée. Of course, if all else failed, I always could call my husband at the office and get on-the-spot advice. But when this happened, Bill knew he had better review that ring binder recipe and revise it for clarity and safety's sake. (I think a few times, my husband dreaded what he might find when he drove home on my cooking night . . . A house burned down all in the service of a perfect flan.)

That ring binder became a resource for a number of us. My husband's daughters would call asking for his recipe for Dominican *Habichuelas.* (Bill had managed what I hadn't managed all my childhood. During our visits to the Island, he had gotten himself invited into the kitchen by my *tías* where he learned how to make *Pastelón,* Sweet-and-Sour Carrots, *Pollo Criollo,* rice with lemon peel, and other things.) A friend wanted to know about Mom's pizza. How did she make that crust? One of my husband's patients would complain that she had more carrots than she could shake a stick at. How about making some Carrot-Ginger Soup and freezing it in containers? Mid-January, what a pleasure to lift the lid of that thawed soup and bring back the summer garden! His mother wanted to know his heart-healthy version of making oven-baked "French fries." Bill would copy that particular recipe and return it to the binder.

But he was no proud and preening chef. When he ate at someone's house and admired a certain dish, he'd ask for the recipe, try it out, then type his variation and put it in the binder. Slowly that binder grew, and you can imagine what began to happen. Requests came from those who ate at Bill's table that he either make that binder available to them, or have them over more often to dinner. There are limits to how much entertaining we can do.

I think what made Bill finally decide to turn the binder into a cookbook was when his daughters graduated from college and were out on their own. He worried that they might not eat well or nourish themselves in the ways he knew were important. And so for Christmas one year, he sat down and pulled the recipes from his binder into a book that included his thoughts, stories, anecdotes, and philosophy of cooking, a legacy to pass on to them. He wanted the cookbook to be wholesome, simple, and straightforward. (Remember, many of these recipes had been "tested" on a total cooking oaf.)

Finally, Bill wanted the cookbook to reflect the traditions of *his* childhood, growing up on a Nebraska farm, where cooking began with seeds you put in the ground. Not that every cook has to be a farmer, too, but they can share the same attitudes: a commitment to the land, to wholesome fresh foods, to nourishing others in a way that turns a meal into a communion. Around the table in Papillion, Nebraska, the act of breaking bread together was a ritual that brought together the family and took in the stranger who happened by. All were welcomed at the Eichner table. Forty-five years later, around the table of a different kind of family, melded out of different traditions and pasts, sharing a meal together can still provide a sense of connection and love.

And so, in middle age, I finally learned to cook. This book was my primer. Bill, its author, was my teacher. I am living proof that one can learn to cook from a good cookbook. So maybe my weary mother was not so off the culinary mark when she shooed me out of the kitchen and told me to go do something useful, like read a book.

WHY I WROTE THIS BOOK

Sometime during her first year at Kenyon College, my daughter Sara called home asking, "Papa, how is it you make the red beans?" And Berit, my younger daughter, toward the end of her freshman year at Bates, asked me, "Papa, how is it you make your style of roast chicken?"

I was touched and surprised by these telephone requests. Surprised that they were making the effort to cook at all when they had cafeteria meals available. Touched that they were inquiring about recipes for healthy, basic kinds of foods. Surprised that they had asked me, when after all, their mother's cooking ability and repertoire made mine pale by comparison. And in the end, touched to realize that the food they had eaten around our table really did hold some special place in their memory.

After the surprise of these first calls, with subsequent requests for brownies or bread pudding or *channa* or even Grandma's pizza, I started to feel a deep sense of enjoyment and an affirmation as a father when I was able to supply my daughters with family recipes and minor cooking tips. The answers to all their requests came from my little black two-ring binder of typed recipes, so it was easy to move to the idea that I should compile a version for my children that could serve them as they made the transition from child-at-home through college-student-in-the-dormitory to adult-out-in-the-world-on-your-own.

I doubt either Sara or Berit will ever make cooking part of their profession, either for the public or for their families (as their mother did and my mother did), but their calls home helped me realize the importance they attached to well-cooked and lovingly presented food.

I hope that this book will inspire not just my daughters—the original audience—but all readers to cherish meal preparation as part of the contentment to be found in each day, and as a means of nurturing those whom you love. Don't worry; as you can see from its size, this is not an encyclopedia about food. Think of it as a small instruction manual. I hope it will be a guide and an inspiration for you as well as a ready reference when you want to find out about those old familiar recipes. I hope you will personalize it with your own notes and contradict my assertions with what you know better from your own experience. I hope you will tuck in a few favorite recipes that you accumulate over the years. I hope this book will help you to make food preparation as easy a routine as brushing your teeth, as comforting as picking up a well-thumbed novel from your favorite writer. By the same token, discovering a new recipe or trying a new version of an old one can be just as exciting as finding a new favorite painting or song.

All of which brings me to the question of who I am, and why I feel brave enough to present a book to a larger audience than my immediate circle of family and friends. Truth is, I feel as though I was born with a legacy for bringing food to the table. I was born in Nebraska farm country, to be fed and led and tutored by the best cook in Sarpy County. (For those who are neither beef eaters nor college football fans, Nebraska lies somewhere between Long Island and San Francisco, supporting 416 miles of Interstate 80, formerly known as the Oregon Trail.) Little in terms of Nebraska farm recipes from my childhood is worth passing on to you. But because my legacy for food production that has evolved over forty years began there, I hope my family's story will have something of value as you find yourself on your own in the kitchen.

My mother, Ruth Eichner, found herself on her own in the kitchen at about fifteen years of age. Farming in Nebraska in the 1930s required heavy fueling of men and their teams—twice daily for the horses and four or five times a day for the farmers. As the oldest of six children and the only girl (males only entered the kitchen to eat and rest), her duty was clear.

Ruth decided to excel in her task and improve on the coarse, imprecise methods of her own mother and her immigrant grandmother.

Prior generations of farm cooks relied on neither recipes nor measuring devices, just plenty of lard and butter to lubricate the feeding process. Taking advantage of Betty Crocker and a longer list of ingredients in recipes eventually gained Ruth a reputation as the best cook in Sarpy County.

She shifted gears and quantities when she learned to feed her own brood (her husband plus five kids), with a sharp eye for only the best of new products, techniques, and recipes of the 1940s and 1950s. The production, processing, and delivery of food could have been a full-time job for this partner in share-crop farming, but since "farm wife" meant doing so many jobs back then, she had to learn not to waste food, pennies, or time in cooking. I'm thankful for her belief that boys, too, were allowed to concoct in the kitchen and to experience the nurturing aspect of bringing food to the table. We learned it as a natural part of tilling, planting, harvesting, and husbanding.

The first shock to my farm-based diet came during medical school in the mid-1960s. A breakthrough discovery of the decade was that cholesterol and cigarette smoking shortened lives. Also during medical school, I married my first wife, and found myself living with a woman who had never boiled a potato. So we learned together how to fit meal preparation into two busy professional schedules. Over the next fifteen years, she influenced my diet and cooking experience by becoming an expert in traditional fine cooking. My contribution (in addition to tasting) was to become an expert Vermont gardener.

Two other important ingredients in the evolution of my cooking legacy were the years of periodic living, working, and eating in Third World countries—always with an eye on the garden, market, and kitchen—and then finding myself on my own as I had never been before. Divorced at age forty, I was accustomed to various levels of assisting at meal production, but rarely responsible for the entire operation. I now needed to feed myself every day during an emotionally lonely and tumultuous existence (was it going to last forever?), to provide comforting and nourishing meals for two distraught, early-adolescent daughters (could any food or other form of love really ease their pain?), and to pick up the broken threads of social interaction, which for me had always meant eating at my table.

Finally, starting a new family with a vegetarian partner taught me how unnecessary meat is in a healthy diet. In trying to show Julia how pleasure can be found in cooking and eating, I've learned how diverse, rich, and exciting a vegetarian diet can be.

Although I originally wrote this book for my two daughters, I'm now ready to share it with a larger audience: other daughters, sons, fathers, mothers, widows—anyone really who finds that, either by choice or circumstance, they're on their own in terms of providing nourishment. The seeds for this manual grew out of my personal experience and out of a desire to nurture my daughters as they moved out on their own. But the ideas for recipes and instructions were fleshed out during the hundreds of conversations I have every week with patients in my medical practice in rural Vermont.

Vermonters do tend to be taciturn. We usually start on safe territory—the weather—but once they feel more comfortable, the conversation quickly moves on.

"Is this rain ever going to stop?" a patient might open.

"Probably," I say. "Meanwhile, it sure is good for the sweet corn."

"Yeah, but raspberries aren't worth a darn. It's just another part of a bad year for me. You know my wife died back in March? I don't know if it's ever going to be the same."

"Gosh, no. I guess it won't ever be the same. I suppose now you have to cook for yourself?"

"Yeah, she used to do it all. I just did the garden work. I'm really going to miss her apple pies this fall."

"You know, when I had to start cooking on my own, I was really afraid to try a pie crust for a long time. So I kept working on different kinds of apple crisp until I found a perfect recipe. It's really almost as good as an apple pie, and so much easier. Then a few years later, I tackled pie crusts and found that I can do that too, after a little practice."

Sweet corn season always leads to everybody's own battle with raccoons in the sweet corn patch. I think I've heard every trick out there. But the best story I've heard is about the man who takes his cot out to the middle of the sweet corn patch and sleeps there with a shotgun by his side. That's how important sweet corn is in the Vermont diet. I've also heard every manner of joke about how quickly sweet corn must be cooked after picking in order not to lose any of the natural sweetness. I remember hearing one gardener say that not only must the water be boiling in the kitchen, but you really should start from the far end of the row and pick in the direction of the house so as not to waste any time retracing your steps before the corn reaches the boiling water.

It was just last April when Rose M. was in for a glaucoma check and said, "Here, Ed sent you these onion sets. They're Walla Wallas from Texas. After he planted two hundred, he was all tuckered out, so he thought he'd give you the rest." In the late summer, when Ed was in for his post-op cataract exam, I was happy to tell him that those Walla Wallas were the biggest and sweetest onions I had ever seen. And by the way, would he like to try my onion pie recipe? Ed, a hospital volunteer, had been to my talk about low-fat diets, so he trusted me as a chef as well as an eye doctor, and happily accepted the recipe.

Lots of my older patients with macular degeneration—once they've gotten over the shock of no longer being able to read—will ask about "the special vitamins" advertised for macular degeneration (such as Ocuvites). I reply that their value is not really proven. Furthermore, I explain, in theory they work because of their antioxidant effect. But these same antioxidants—vitamins A, C, and E—can be obtained in a healthy diet. Just remember to include leafy greens, carrots, and beans. "In fact," I say, "have you ever tried kale soup? I'd love to share with you a recipe from my friend Devon. It was passed down to her by relatives in Illinois, from ancestors in Denmark."

Just last week, Rosemary C. asked what I knew about Mexican pizza. She explained that she'd been given some "flat, white, floury Mexican things" and was told they would work for Mexican pizza. "Oh," I said, "you must mean flour tortillas. They'll work great for making burritos. Just roll some diced cooked potatoes, red or black beans, and browned onions into the tortilla, and heat them in the oven. Plus, you can use your own homemade salsa on top. They'll work great for your diabetic and low-fat diet, Rosemary." I could see that I had made a plug for personal health care that she had really heard. As I was leaving the room she asked, "Will making burritos help my eyes, too?"

So you see how the conversations go. Sometimes, they are emotional, heart-to-heart talks about tragic life transitions: the death of a partner, a painful divorce, or a downturn in financial circumstances. Other times, we just deal with the facts of life about putting food on the table. Food costs money, cooking sometimes gets boring, and there's always the question of what is the best way to eat well and stay healthy. And I hear statements of intense reluctance, "I hate to cook!" or, "But I don't know *how* to cook. How can I ever find the time?" And then the kind of question that expresses both an interest and a lack of confidence, "How do I make it healthy?" And sometimes simply a statement of frustration, "But I don't *like* spinach."

In the end, whether we feel fears and frustrations about food and cooking or not, we have to understand that it is a universal habit, just like breathing. I guess breathing is a bit more automatic, but really eating is sort of an automatic habit too, so long as someone puts a plate in front of us. What I want to address in this book is the challenge of moving past the automatic part and *taking charge* of what you put in your mouth. Whether you're plunged abruptly into the need to be on your own in the kitchen, or make this a leisurely choice because of new interests and new desires, you'll most certainly need some background instructions and a collection of recipes that work for you from week to week.

I wouldn't think of prescribing a diet for you. A diet is way too personal. In the end, you'll do that for yourself, depending on where you live, your taste for certain foods, your financial circumstances, and the time you can put into meal planning and execution. Instead, my prescription is that you should use this cookbook as you develop your own personal food style. Refer to it every day when you think about how you're going to feed yourself.

After thirty years of doctoring, cooking, and eating, I'm offering this manual to guide you, not only to nutritional health but also to find pleasure in preparing and consuming good-tasting meals. Read on. The words are few but the task is long. I promise to help you learn to make nutritious choices, to acquire wholesome, appealing ingredients, and to make cooking challenging and exciting enough that you won't mind thinking about it every day.

However my own cooking legacy evolves over the next few decades, I hope this manual will be an incentive for you to develop your own cooking history. Whether your eating style evolves just from necessity or from an excitement about food, and whether that food comes from the garden or from the market shelf, I hope you always find food a source of nourishment, of health, of quality, and of joy in your life and the lives of those you nurture.

CHAPTER ONE

GETTING STARTED

E VERY SUCCESSFUL MEAL (that means fun to prepare and satis-
fying to consume) starts before you find yourself standing in the
kitchen with your apron on. The kitchen has to be equipped and ingredients have to be at hand.

If you're starting with a bare kitchen, go out today and shop for
some essentials so that you can eat tomorrow. Unless you're living
forty miles from the market, you don't have to stock your kitchen for
the next month. In most of the world, cooks shop for one day at a
time. Not only does this mean you can plan for one day's eating at a
time, but you can keep your ingredients fresh.

ESSENTIAL EQUIPMENT AND INGREDIENTS

For equipment, too, don't try to get everything you'll use for the rest
of your life. The embellishments can be added over months and
years as your skills and enjoyment of the art expand. Besides, when
you visit relatives, friends, or yard sales, you may find some handy
items for free or next to free. In fact, I've thought of planning an "on-
your-own shower" for my daughters. That is, a little party to which
friends can bring some pieces of kitchen equipment.

When you head out for your first equipment-shopping trip, here
are some things to consider. You don't have to start with a 400-pound
solid maple butcher block, even though one happens to be the real
center of my kitchen. Instead, find yourself a hardwood (that means

maple) cutting board that you can place on your counter for chopping and cutting without worrying about damaging your countertop. For the other end of the cutting process, I suggest you have two knives. Find an inexpensive stainless steel paring knife. These cost about five dollars apiece, so you can eventually have a half-dozen of them, all in different shapes. The more substantial knife you'll need is a chef's knife, with a blade at least 8 to 10 inches long. This is the instrument you'll rely on for all your chopping, cutting, slicing, and dicing. A good one does mean a substantial investment, but I would like to put in a plug for the high-carbon steel variety that costs about half the price of stainless steel. Besides the economy, the high-carbon steel blade allows you the opportunity to sharpen it yourself. (Use a wood- or plastic-handled sharpener that contains two gritty sharpening wheels. Just pull the blade between the wheels a dozen times to make a new sharp edge.) Don't worry about the dark color that the blade develops over time. This is just oxidation and is easily removed with a little lemon juice. You may have to look hard to find this type of chef's knife, but it will last a lifetime with minimal care.

For the stovetop, I suggest you find at least one nonstick frying pan, preferably two inches deep with a lid. T-FAL is a reliable brand. I used to think that cast iron was the only way to sauté, but seasoning and maintaining the pans really isn't worth it. Still, if you want to start as a purist, you can easily find cast iron for low prices at yard sales and auctions.

Look for a good 2-quart saucepan with a lid for making rice, cooking sauces, and other uses. Stainless steel is the best material, unless you've just come into some big money and can afford copper. It's important that the bottom be heavy, with an internal layer of aluminum or copper for even heating. The same goes for the next larger cooking pot, a 3- to 5-quart, wide-diameter (8 to 10 inches), two-handled, covered casserole or stew pot. Don't forget one or two 9-by-12-inch Pyrex baking dishes and a 10-inch pie plate.

The final, and really essential piece of cookware is a big stockpot. Even if you don't make your own stock, you'll need this for cooking pasta, simmering soup, and making enough red beans to have some all week. The size depends on your needs. Be sure that it holds at least 8 quarts, and 12 quarts is not excessive. More important than size is workmanship. Stainless steel will again put you in the medium price range. Be sure to find one with an aluminum or copper layer in the base for good conduction and maintenance of heat. Even though you will generally use this pot for cooking liquids, there will be times when you will brown or sauté certain ingredients before the liquids are added.

Mixing tools range from a whisk for a few dollars to a hand-held electric beater to a more expensive KitchenAid mixer. The latter is a nice luxury for mixing bread dough, homemade pasta, and cakes. The KitchenAid brand indicates that the mixer will be a reliable old workhorse. In fact, I have Grandma Eichner's mixer, which is over twenty years old, and it is still a solid machine. You know there is an upscale device for chopping and grating as well—namely the food processor. I use my Cuisinart a lot, but if you're on a tight budget, your chef's knife and an old-style four-sided grater will handle most jobs with only a little more time needed.

Consider purchasing a small toaster oven (in the $30 to $40 range) for heating small quantities of food without firing up a full-size oven. I know microwave ovens are much more popular, and I believe they really are useful for quick thawing of food (that you forgot to take out of the freezer 12 hours ahead of time) or rewarming a cold cup of coffee. In fact, I have experience with a microwave oven at the office, which I use every day for quickly heating my lunch. But I have to be very careful to heat bread no more than 15 seconds, and my lunch for no more than 60 seconds, or I end up with something inedible. At home, I much prefer the toaster oven because it enhances the texture and maintains the flavor of food during the heating, rather than destroying them. We use ours every morning for a slow, low-heat thawing of a frozen homemade roll. In the end, it tastes and feels like it just came from the original baking in the oven. We also use it every night when our dinner consists of leftovers. It's great for roasting a red pepper or grilling a portabello mushroom, without having to turn on the big oven.

You'll need to acquire lots of smaller items. A set of glass measuring cups should include 1 cup, 1 pint, and 1 quart. A set of hard plastic ones, including ¼ cup, ⅓ cup, ½ cup, and 1 cup are also essential. You'll need a set or two of measuring spoons, a hardwood rolling pin (at least 18 inches long, cylindrical, without handles), some baking sheets, cooling racks, a dough scraper or two, a garlic press, a colander (for draining pasta and washing vegetables), a stainless steel swivel peeler (the

Good Grips brand has revolutionized this little instrument), a collection of wooden spoons, a couple of hard plastic spoons and spatulas to use with your nonstick pan, plenty of durable, easy-wash mixing bowls (I like Pyrex), a small strainer, and a small flour sifter. The list can go on and on, but I think these are the essentials.

You'll also need to stock some basic ingredients. Include flour (all-purpose, unbleached), sugar (white, brown, and confectioners'), cooking oil (canola and inexpensive olive), vinegar, lemon juice, vanilla extract, cubes of vegetable or chicken bouillon, salt, pepper, and a list of the spices and herbs that most appeal to you (go easy here since they do get stale), cocoa, cornmeal, baking soda, baking powder, rice, beans (kidney, pinto, black), dried pasta, onions, garlic, and gingerroot. Also make a list of perishables to get you started. For the refrigerator, at the minimum you'll need eggs, milk, butter, and, for my taste, a chunk of Parmesan cheese. This list of ingredients is by no means complete, but if you start with this, and sit down with a recipe book to begin planning some meals, I think you will find that your kitchen is pretty well stocked.

COOKING BY THE SEASONS AND THE SEASONINGS

As you plan menus and make shopping lists, keep the season of the year in mind. For those of you who live in New England, you know what "season" means. Here in Vermont we have at least four distinct ones. If you develop the passion for eating, cooking, and gardening that I have, you'll learn that seasons really play into the choices we make.

Spring happens to be my favorite season. This is when my annual gardening/cooking cycle starts over again. Three important food markers for spring are asparagus, spinach, and rhubarb. I happily wait all year for them to appear in my own garden or our own farmers' market, rather than make do with the "off-season" products available from Florida or Mexico. Travel doesn't enhance the flavor of fruits or vegetables.

Summer, with all its splendor, variety, and abundance of produce, seems almost excessive. I spend all my energy harvesting and using up these seasonal gifts or trying to put them away to bring out again as a reminder on some cold, dark winter night. Highlights of summer include raspberries, new potatoes, *haricots vert* (French green beans), the first tiny zucchini, cucumbers hanging long and thin from the trellis, and mounds of fresh basil (the aroma filling the kitchen). Later on we harvest yellow and red peppers, tomatoes picked at their peak of ripeness on a sunny day, and finally sweet corn, at its finest only if you can bring it from your own patch immediately to the boiling water and then to the table.

By autumn, the flavor of the summer vegetables intensifies a bit with cooler nights and shorter days. Raspberries are still abundant. Tomatoes are still plentiful, but we know that their season may end any day with the first killing frost. It's time to start harvesting one of our all-time favorites, the beautiful and versatile leek. We dig the rest of the carrots, and store the winter squash and pumpkins as we go through the short transition of autumn and start to plan for the long, dark winter ahead. Autumn became easier for me when I learned this was a second season in the year to enjoy leafy greens (arugula, broadleaf cress, spinach, and various lettuces and endives). Autumn is like a brief return to spring before the garden season finally comes to a stop. When it does, the menus and meal plans take on quite a different shape.

Winter is the time to start thinking of hearty casseroles, flavorful soups, and other slow-cooking recipes. This is the season when we have more time for preparation, and we don't mind if our cooking heats up the kitchen.

I guess if you're a gardener as well as a cook, the importance of seasons to the art of cooking comes to you automatically after you go through a few cycles. But even if you rely on the market, the availability, prices, and quality will all be better if you use seasonal produce.

Once you buy (or grow) a food product that you believe is at its peak of flavor, your task is to preserve and enhance that flavor as you prepare it for the table. I like raw vegetables, but not arranged on a plate, pretending to be a meal. Raw vegetables taste best eaten in the garden. Just brush the soil or mulch off a carrot, and try the tomato still covered with morning dew. The advantages of the raw vegetable are its visual appeal, nutrient value, texture, and flavor. These are the elements that you'll want to retain while you cook the vegetables. This means cooking for the shortest possible time (to a tender, crisp state), and going light on seasoning so as not to mask the natural flavors. Keep the cooking oil to a minimum, and serve food immediately after cooking.

GOOD FOOD MEANS A GOOD GARDEN

Somehow, in order to fully enjoy the process of putting food on the table every day, we need to make a connection with a garden, or gardeners, or a farmers' market. The supermarket is such a cruel thief when it comes to quality in food. The finest chefs in the world certainly don't empty their pockets in a supermarket, so why should you? It's enough to shell out for the everyday, unalterable staples (for us anyway) like milk and orange juice. Nowhere in this treatise will I persuade you to milk cows or grow oranges. (Although I did once own milk cows and will admit to you that I aspire to have my own orange grove so that I can bring a fresh supply of juice to my beloved every morning.)

Relying on the supermarket for fruits and vegetables will surely rob you of that ultimate pleasure of tasting a tomato or a cantaloupe or a pear at its most succulent ripeness. Yes, if these things are picked in their greenest state from a commercial farm across the country from your table, they will eventually soften on their path to decomposition, but they'll never be *ripe*.

So, back to an alternative. Perhaps, in order to avoid all the costly packaging on the supermarket shelf and to protect against the unknown chemicals that have affected the supermarket vegetables, fruits, and grains (is it still a grain when it has been super-refined, bleached, and sterilized?), and to taste the meaning of "locally ripened," we should consider involving ourselves earlier with the food we consume. Might we acquaint ourselves directly with the grower and ask about her philosophy of quality and safety of the produce, about the methods used to produce quality foods?

After a few trips to a local farmers' market, you will learn that green beans can be crisp and slender and flavorful. That lettuce comes in many colors and flavors and textures, all of which are distinguishable if it hasn't traveled two thousand miles in a cardboard box. That carrots and potatoes can be so fresh that you won't need to peel them. That cucumbers taste better when they aren't coated in wax. In fact, almost every vegetable or fruit grown within a fifty-mile radius and eaten in its season will be noticeably superior to the commercial products that come from factory farms a long way from your table.

Taste a few local garden products and you may even be tempted to the ultimate trip—raising your own. For me, no eating experience can compare to the first salad of our garden's season, when I bring in a basket of just-cut arugula and broadleaf cress along with two or three early lettuce varieties (Red Sails, Black Seeded Simpson, Oak Leaf), none of the leaves more than two inches high. Any dressing "stronger" than lemon juice and olive oil would mask the mix of barely developed flavors: bitter, peppery, and tangy. On the other hand, you might prefer the sensual delight of harvesting your own asparagus spears—which only emerged from the soil in the past twenty-four hours—trying to decide whether the thick ones steamed for five minutes are as tasty as the thin ones steamed for three to four minutes. Don't add anything but a squeeze of lemon juice.

Or is the season's first spinach your ultimate delight? You didn't realize spinach could be so filled with flavor before "aging" in transport or storage. Or you might be hooked on a tomato that reaches its full ripeness before you pick it and eat it in the garden. Or potatoes that you dig when they are the size of small eggs, or sweet corn so fresh that it really is sweet.

Think about how you can make this closer connection to the source of the food you choose to eat. You may not have the luxury of a large garden space or years of "farmer experience" as I have, but why not use a corner of your suburban lawn, or a piece of a friend's lawn, a community garden spot, or even some large pots or boxes on the terrace or balcony? Once you experience this connection, you will never again be satisfied with "plastic produce"—the stuff that was picked before it developed flavor and is therefore worn out before the time you buy it. You will become a discriminating shopper willing to pay a little more, or travel a few more blocks, or work at growing your own. Just remember that, when you are on your own, it may take more time and effort. The payoffs will be increased pleasure in consuming vegetables and fruits that taste good, and better health because you'll want to make vegetables and fruits the major part of your diet.

Just in case you are still a glutton for meat, you should know that the same concepts also hold for animal products. I've had the experience of raising chickens (and loving their truly fresh eggs), rabbits, turkeys, lambs, veal, beef, and even the despicable hog. When I first sampled these products at the table, it was clear that the taste, quality, and freshness of meat that came from our own farm was clearly superior to anything I could buy in the supermarket. I am planning to raise our own chickens and rabbits on the farm we bought in the Dominican Republic, so that they can feed on the scraps from the organic garden. And we can occasionally add meat to the *sancocho, si Dios quiere* (stew, if God wishes).

My daughter, Berit, was around one recent summer to share in a bit of the bounty of our huge summer-long fruit production. I can't tell you how happy that made me. She could attest to the splendor of the Bosc pears (I didn't know they could be grown in Vermont either), and the several varieties of hard, tart, cooking-type apples. Unfortunately, Berit left before the peaches were ready to pick, and several varieties of later apples ripened after her visit—not to mention the overabundance of cantaloupe from the late-summer garden. In fact, this represented the first real fruit harvest that I can brag about after twenty years of planting fruit trees in Vermont (and moving from house to house). Yet I would go through the same thing again for just one harvest such as we enjoyed that summer. Oh, how easily and how grandly is the tree-planter rewarded. Good rootstock, knowing how to put a sapling into the soil, some sun and water, and a lot of patience—that's all it takes. *¡Gracias a Dios!*

Seasoning, which means enhancing the food's natural flavor, is an art that you will perfect over time. If your main ingredients are of high quality, use only a little salt or pepper or fresh lemon juice at the end of the cooking process to enhance that natural flavor. *Flavoring* (adding a new taste to a food) is meant to modify the original flavor. To be successful, you will need to familiarize yourself not only with the aroma and flavor of the herbs and spices you like, but also with how they affect the food. Make sure spices are fresh when you buy them, don't buy too large a quantity, and go easy until you have experienced the effect in your recipes. Many natural food stores sell spices in bulk, so you can buy small amounts of several for testing. Spices also tend to be fresher in this setting. My favorites include allspice, basil, cardamom, cinnamon, cloves, coriander (called cilantro when you're using the leaf rather than the seed), cumin, garlic, ginger, nutmeg, and rosemary. Have fun exploring and make your own list of favorites.

A NOTE ON MEASURING

Since there is a little science associated with the art of cooking, a few words about measuring are probably in order. Good cakes and pastries require precise measurements of ingredients. But please don't obsess with exactness when you're making soups, beans, marinara, pasta, and sauces. Most recipes will provide some guidelines, but remember, you're preparing the food for your own taste, so don't be afraid to rely on your judgment. If your first try wasn't quite right, you can always make an adjustment the next time around. In some cases (homemade bread for instance), you will have to vary the amount of flour or water from one week to the next, depending on the ambient temperature and humidity.

It is helpful to have some minimal knowledge of equivalent measurements and conversions. For instance, you need to know that an ounce may mean either $\frac{1}{16}$ of a pound, or $\frac{1}{16}$ of a pint. One refers to weight and the other to volume, but there is no relationship between the two. This is an unfortunate aspect to our U.S. (and also the British) system of measurement. In the metric system, there are relationships between weight and volume, which are very handy. Since our predicted turnover to the metric system has yet to begin, I'll only bother you with some useful equivalents in our own U.S. volume system.

1 tablespoon	= 3 teaspoons
	= $\frac{1}{2}$ fluid ounce
4 tablespoons	= $\frac{1}{4}$ cup
	= 2 fluid ounces
16 tablespoons	= 1 cup
	= 8 fluid ounces

And in case you've forgotten:

2 cups	= 1 pint
	= ½ quart
	= 16 fluid ounces
4 cups	= 1 quart
	= 32 fluid ounces
4 quarts	= 1 gallon

Incidentally:

1 quart	= 1.06 liters (nearly equivalent)
1 kilogram	= 2.2 pounds = 1,000 grams
1 pound	= 454 grams (slightly less than ½ kilogram)

What fun we'll have with kitchen conversions if we ever do make the switch to metric!

One final tip: go out and buy the new edition of *Joy of Cooking* by Rombauer and Becker. Take it home and put it on your kitchen shelf. Every time a question comes up either from this cookbook or from some other recipe you're using, or when you'd like to know something more about a particular food or ingredient, remember that encyclopedic text on your shelf and pull it down. You'll find a wealth of information about ingredients, basic foods, cooking techniques, and hundreds of recipes, all presented in a manner that is a delight to read. You may find as I do that *Joy of Cooking* is the "bible" when you need depth and breadth. But I hope that this book will be your daily sourcebook of recipes that you'll use every time you plan a menu or prepare to cook one of your favorites.

Now it's time. So yes, let's get started! Check out the brief essays in this book (highlighted with borders). They're meant to inspire you and help you through your fears. (In other words, imagine that I'm there to talk you through this.) Then check out the recipes and choose a couple for your first weekend in the kitchen on your own. Wait a few weeks to try homemade pasta or homemade bread, until your confidence has grown through experience. Choose something that appeals to your taste and sense of adventure. Remember, adventure is part of the enjoyment in this process we call cooking.

MAKING MISTAKES IN THE KITCHEN

by Julia Alvarez

As Bill often reminds me, some recipes are more forgiving than others.

I'll say. The time I did not put sugar in the brownies, the brownie-eaters were not forgiving. Dear Bill offered to eat them bitter with a pile of sweet ice cream on top, but I think there are certain things a person should not do, even for love.

The time I misread the Date Chocolate-Chip recipe, the cake turned out very dry, very unforgiving. I still claim that error wasn't all my fault. The little black ring binder, which was the earlier incarnation of this cookbook, read: *put chopped dates in one & ½ c. of water.* Now, you tell me, if it does not make perfect sense, especially when the ampersand is kind of faded, to read, *one ½ cup,* and only put in half a cup of water?

"But why would I put in *one* half cup?" Bill argued back. "As opposed to *two* half cups?! That's one cup!"

Kitchens, by the way, are great places to test your marriage.

Well, I've forgiven him for the clumsy entry in that old ring binder, and he's forgiven me for the dry cake, and we've both learned to be more careful. Especially when you are sharing your recipes with someone else, you do have to remember your shorthand might not translate well. Thus the usefulness of a carefully proofread manual like this one.

I also admit that until you learn the language of cooking, it is like a foreign tongue you need to practice. I've learned to pay better attention in order to become fluent in certain procedures and recipes. Bill and his mom still smile when they remember my talking to Molly O'Neill about their old family recipe for Christmas supper after church.

"Chili and oyster stew?" Molly curled up her nose. Even though, like Bill's family, Molly is a native of Nebraska, and she has traveled all over the world, and she had never heard of such a mixture.

Thank goodness Mom and Bill were sitting right there during this interview of "writers who cook" and explained on my behalf, "We didn't mix them together, of course. The kids had chili and the grownups ate oyster stew."

Of course.

I sat at that table very quietly, as if I had known all along that these were two separate recipes. But to be truthful, I had misheard Bill and his mom's description for years. I actually thought they mixed their chili with their oyster stew. I was awfully glad to find out Nebraskans were not as weird as all that.

Misread or misheard recipes have plagued me a bit. But the only errors I've made recently (in the kitchen) have been teensy and forgivable. Nothing at all in the scope of a recent *Washington Post* recipe for Beef Tenderloin that asked for "2 pounds baby, stems removed and discarded." Now I would probably never make Beef Tenderloin, since I am a vegetarian, but had I come across this recipe in that old ring binder, I am sure I would have called Bill up at the office to let him know that there are certain things a person shouldn't cook, even for love.

CHAPTER TWO

COMMON SENSE, HEALTH, AND EATING

EVER SINCE I BECAME A PHYSICIAN, I have relied on scientific method to guide me in my profession, and I use it every day to help me in making choices for my patients. I find that I often rely on this method, though not in a particularly conscious way, to make choices in other areas of my life as well, especially around matters of personal health, lifestyle, and, of course, about eating. You probably remember from school that the scientific method of testing goes hand-in-hand with statistics. We present and then test a hypothesis. In most cases, we are happy if we end up with an acceptable "confidence level," a desirable level of probability. True scientific method reminds us that we must always leave room in our conclusion for further evidence that may finally prove our hypothesis wrong.

I've come to believe, however, after thirty-plus years as an adult, that this method is not always adequate for making long-term choices. I've seen too many facts finally reversed and discarded. When my children were young, I read so much "evidence" that sugar ingestion caused hyperactivity in susceptible kids that I almost came to believe it. As you probably know, in recent years this theory has been thrown out as bunk. Likewise the craze for vitamin supplements. By today's standards, an excess of vitamins can be bad for you. There are plenty of other examples of "facts" becoming fiction. What I now realize is that choices about things as basic as what we eat have to include other kinds of reasoning in addition to the scientific method.

Yes, I read and compare articles, test hypotheses against things that I know. I try to be patient about trying fads or accepting anecdotal evidence. But in the end, I've made personal choices, not every one of which is based on evidence. In medical practice, too, we make a lot of studied decisions that are based on relatively few absolute (proven) truths.

So I can't give you a scientific recipe for living a healthy life. I only want to guide you in how you go about making your own choices about eating as part of your lifestyle.

And now, I will tell you in capsule form what I do and what works for me. Most of what makes up my style of eating and food preparation came about by serendipity over the years. I can think of only a few absolute choices I made. For instance, I decided at age forty to start a regular program of aerobic exercise. Another decision was to stop smoking forever at age forty-one. But it was only slowly that I came to realize that my new diet was probably most closely patterned after Mediterranean cuisine. Such a diet includes a reliance on grains and seasonal vegetables. The Mediterranean diet is generally low in fat (except for monounsaturated oils such as olive and canola), includes seafood when it's available in a fresh state, and only the occasional use of red meat.

It is a fact that some types of heart disease are caused by the buildup of atheromatous, or fatty plaques in cardiac vessels. It's not proven that this buildup is related to cholesterol in the diet. Yet we find evidence in many studies that some kind of relationship exists between diet and atheromatous disease. One oft-repeated example of a cause-and-effect relationship portrays the Mediterranean-style diet as beneficial in terms of preventing heart disease. Yet, even now, we have to be prepared for new ideas that may come along to upset our confidence.

In addition to relying on science, I must admit to occasionally relying on anecdotal evidence. My father is a perfect example of an "anecdote" that I use as "evidence." Because of changes in lifestyle, mostly in his eating habits, he's far more robust now as he approaches eighty than he was in his late fifties. After he moved to Vermont and he and I finally had a chance to forge a closer relationship, I was able to urge him to try a low-fat diet. He has enthusiastically built upon the few suggestions I made, and now exercises regularly, eats sensibly, and has finally been told by his doctor to throw away the medications that he has used for many years to treat diabetes and high blood pressure. Statistically this anecdote means nothing, but I only hope that we can all be as lucky as my father.

So keep your eyes and ears open concerning new evidence and new trends, but don't be afraid to stick with what you feel is best for you. Bring in changes when you are ready, with the idea that they might make your diet style more adventurous and tasty, as well as improving your long-term health.

SCIENCE ENTERS IN

My daughter Sara asked me to supply her with a table indicating which foods would be sources for certain nutrients. Her request sent me to the library. And my reading brought up a lot of technical material that I need to pass along, so please indulge me in some technical talk. After all, I am a doctor, so I want to give you some scientific basis for everything I'm trying to share in this cookbook.

Some poets think the eyes are windows to the soul. Traditional and homeopathic healers do an external examination of the eyes to determine the health of patients. Ophthalmologists peer through the pupil to examine blood vessels in living, pulsing color for subtle signs of disease states and for an impression of the health of the vascular system. So even as "eye doctors," we care about and evaluate the general health of our patients while we look through our special windows.

When I graduated from medical school thirty years ago, I had not taken one course in nutrition. We had a course called Epidemiology and Preventive Medicine that we all laughed about because the course didn't teach us how to cure disease. In fact, it dealt with statistics and probabilities. We learned how to look at a hypothesis to see whether it really "proved" anything. We also heard about the Framingham study—something to do with the risk factors for heart disease.

In later years, I changed my mind about this "useless" course. After years in postgraduate and fellowship training and a stint in the Air Force, I finally found myself in private practice. Two weeks into my first job, I was faced with an acute outbreak of food poisoning in a cloistered population of two thousand people. I looked around, but I found no one else to turn to. And then I thought back to a two-lecture series in the epidemiology course about a salmonellosis outbreak at a Methodist-Episcopal church picnic. I set to work. Within forty-eight hours, I had identified the source of the toxin—sure enough, a salad containing eggs. The outbreak was corralled, everyone recovered, and the group resumed business as usual. I had just participated in investigative epidemiology and won a round.

RX: RECIPES

by Julia Alvarez

Often when patients find out that Bill cooks, they look at me in shock, "Your husband is a doctor *and* he cooks?"

This is not quite the same as the shock of my old Dominican *tías* when they find out my husband cooks. In their minds, being a man and being a cook are mutually exclusive categories. As one very religious old aunt explained to me, "You never see Jesus cooking in the Bible do you?"

I searched my memory for some little recollection from years of studying the gospels in parochial school. There was the instance of the loaves and the fishes, Christ feeding the multitudes by multiplying a couple of loaves, a handful of fish.

"*Bueno,*" my *tía* conceded, that was an instance of our Lord involved in food preparation of a kind. "But why do you think that they call it a miracle?"

Of course, my old *tía* had a smile on her lips. Men who cook, even Dominican men who cook, are not such an anomaly anymore. In the States, men have been cooking since the barbecue and suburbs were invented! And of course, since the women's movement, men have migrated indoors to kitchens, where they not only cook but mop the floors and do the dishes.

But a doctor who cooks. . . . Why does this still cause surprise in some quarters? Perhaps it's just the surprise and delight we feel when we encounter multitalented people: professors who have apple orchards, car mechanics who are expert fly fishermen. But cooking and medicine are actually kindred professions. Not quite the oxymoronic leap we must take to imagine a poet who sells life insurance, say. (Though Wallace Stevens did both!) Cooking and doctoring have long been allied. I discovered just how deep this alliance goes when I realized that the word for prescription in Spanish, *receta,* is the same as the word for recipe, *receta.*

A recipe and a prescription—the kindred root of these two activities still survives in English in the form of the abbreviation "Rx" for medical prescriptions. The word first came into usage circa 1584, borrowed from the Latin *recipe!* or "take!"—the imperative of *recipere*: to take, to receive. The sense of instructions for preparing food did not appear until 1743.

And so, each recipe can be a kind of preventive prescription, for a wholesome dish with farm-fresh ingredients cooked in a heart-healthy way that can keep you fit and out of the doctor's office. A recipe a day keeps the doctor away.

Unless, of course, the doctor is also the cook!

As years went on, I found that all the jargon—"retrospective" versus "prospective," "student t test," "confidence level," "outcomes and probabilities"—became practical tools for me, both in my profession and in my daily life. With these tools, I learned to sift through and evaluate all the data, both professional and popular, that passes under my reading lamp. I gained the confidence I needed to try new surgical methods and new styles of diet.

Evaluating data is valuable in making choices that result in one's "health-style" and even a "food-style." Incidentally, *style* is defined as a quality of imagination and individuality, expressed in one's actions and tastes. So I do think that we all eventually develop a style in our approach to health as well as a style in how we deal with food and eating.

If you're not aware that you have a food-style, stop and think about it. You may be unaware of having one because your eating style is as automatic to you as your breathing style. For example, lunch every day might consist of a bag of potato chips or French fries and a Big Mac. If so, it doesn't mean you don't have a food-style, just that you haven't thought about it. (If your food-style really is that bad, it's time to hit this book hard and think about some changes.)

Is my health-style and food-style better than yours? Is the diet that fits my food-style ideal? Of course not. There can be many varieties of healthy styles of eating. I would just ask you to look at improving some of the elements of your style that might contribute to long-term health and nutrition.

The U.S. Department of Agriculture and the U.S. Department of Health and Human Services periodically update and release a set of Dietary Guidelines for Americans. These guidelines are meant to provide information based on current medical and nutrition research. These are the latest ones, published in January 2000:

1. Aim for a healthy weight.
2. Be physically active each day.
3. Let the pyramid guide your food choices.
4. Choose a variety of grains daily, especially whole grains.
5. Choose a variety of fruits and vegetables daily.
6. Keep food safe to eat.

7. Choose a diet that is low in saturated fat and cholesterol and moderate in total fat.
8. Choose beverages and foods that limit your intake of sugars.
9. Choose and prepare foods with less salt.
10. If you drink alcoholic beverages, do so in moderation.

Food Guide Pyramid

A Guide to Daily Food Choices

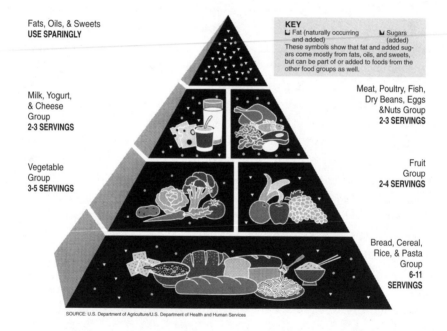

Fats, Oils, & Sweets
USE SPARINGLY

KEY
◻ Fat (naturally occurring and added)   ▾ Sugars (added)
These symbols show that fat and added sugars come mostly from fats, oils, and sweets, but can be part of or added to foods from the other food groups as well.

Milk, Yogurt, & Cheese Group
2-3 SERVINGS

Meat, Poultry, Fish, Dry Beans, Eggs & Nuts Group
2-3 SERVINGS

Vegetable Group
3-5 SERVINGS

Fruit Group
2-4 SERVINGS

Bread, Cereal, Rice, & Pasta Group
6-11 SERVINGS

SOURCE: U.S. Department of Agriculture/U.S. Department of Health and Human Services

Before examining these and other guidelines, it's probably time to discuss some terms and basic concepts about food chemistry and nutrition.

Virtually all the food we eat consists of either carbohydrates, proteins, or fats. Each class of food is necessary, in varying proportions, to maintain life. We tend to think of proteins as building blocks, fats as stored energy, and carbohydrates as the basic fuel for energy production. Even though the body can convert any of these three substances to glucose (sugar) whenever there is a demand for energy, other essential elements in fats and proteins cannot be obtained elsewhere, so we can't ignore any of these classes of foods.

We need protein to supply essential amino acids and nitrogen for the structural building and repair of our body tissues. Eight "essential" amino acids have been identified—that is, amino acids that our bodies cannot synthesize from other amino acids. Various foods differ in protein quality depending on their supply of each of these eight amino acids.

Meat, soybeans, spinach, and milk are "complete" proteins, while other high protein legumes are low in two of the amino acids. Grains, however, have opposite strengths and weaknesses, so they complement legumes in meeting the requirement for all eight essential amino acids—a good reason to combine beans and rice. But if we consume a *varied* diet based on the food pyramid, we need not worry over these details—we can easily exceed our requirements for complete proteins.

Fats are also necessary for our health. We use them to transport and store vitamins, as well as to store energy. However, in times of shortage, fats can be manufactured in the body from other calorie sources. Our main concern about dietary fat should be to limit our total intake, with special care to avoid the saturated variety (butter, animal fat, coconut oil) and hydrogenated fats such as margarine.

Carbohydrates deserve more discussion since they occupy such a large part of the food pyramid. Carbohydrates may be *simple*, such as the sucrose of table sugar or the fructose found in fruits. Simple forms of carbohydrates are converted very quickly in the body to glucose, the final fuel element. As a result of this quick conversion, a rapid elevation of blood sugar occurs, requiring a large amount of insulin so the body cells can utilize this bolus of glucose. The calories (energy) may be useful to satisfy a sudden demand for energy, but they are "empty" in terms of other nutritional value.

In contrast, carbohydrates may be *complex,* as exemplified by starchy products such as whole grains, breads, pasta, rice, and vegetables like potatoes. Complex carbohydrates are present in non-starchy vegetables as well. These are broken down into the glucose form over a much longer time period, so have a slower and longer effect on blood sugar level and a correspondingly lower need for insulin to facilitate utilization by the body.

A healthy diet, even for someone with diabetes, should be high in complex carbohydrates, because they supply energy over the long term, usually not requiring drastic adjustments in insulin levels. Simple carbohydrates are bad for people with diabetes, and are of little or no use for the rest of us except in the case of a demand for quick energy.

I hope this helps you understand better some of the terms mentioned in the dietary guidelines.

The medical establishment has been criticized for its lack of interest in nutrition education and for being inconsistent in dietary recommendations that affect health and disease. A notable exception is the Framingham Study, which I heard about in my old Preventive Medicine class. The Framingham Study is an ongoing collection of data from an average community near Boston. The study was designed to seek the factors that are statistically related to heart disease, the nation's number one cause of death and morbidity (the level of sick compared to well people in a given community). It took only thirty years for researchers to reach the conclusion that would help set new dietary guidelines for America: *high blood pressure, high blood cholesterol, and smoking are all serious risk factors for heart disease.*

Evidence from the Framingham Study provides a tool with which we can make lifestyle choices that affect the quality and length of our lives. That is, stop smoking, exercise regularly, and aim toward a diet that will help control blood pressure and blood cholesterol.

Later studies have been inconclusive about the relationship between dietary cholesterol and blood levels of cholesterol. It seems that eating saturated fats that contain no cholesterol can cause elevation of one's blood level of cholesterol, while the ingestion of monounsaturated oils (olive, canola) may have an opposite, beneficial effect on blood cholesterol levels. Despite some controversial conclusions, a consensus common to all the studies links diet and disease. *Diets low in fat, high in complex carbohydrates, and high in fiber seem to be protective for the whole gamut of diseases we hope to avoid: cancer, diabetes, high blood pressure, cardiovascular disease, strokes, osteoporosis, and obesity.* These broad statements still leave a lot of options for individual styles and choices, but now we have some scientific guidelines around which to plan a diet that almost certainly will promote our long-term health and physical well-being.

I've been pleasantly surprised while doing this research to find that people in ophthalmology finally have something to say about nutrition. For example, Dr. Barry Hyman (one of my teachers while I was a resident at Baylor) reports for the National Heart, Lung and Blood Institute that dietary sodium has a direct and dose-dependent effect on blood pressure. The Institute suggests that we moderate our consumption of sodium by avoiding processed foods, increasing the proportion of fruits, vegetables, and legumes in our diet, and adding less salt while cooking and at the table.

Here's another report from the "eye world": Dr. D. Max Snodderly, a researcher at the Schepen Eye Research Institute, published data in 1995 suggesting that dietary carotenoids, by their antioxidant effect, decrease the risk of age-related macular degeneration (the highest cause of visual loss in people over age sixty-five). Studies conducted at five American ophthalmology centers report that adults whose diets contained the most dark-green leafy vegetables were 43 percent less likely to develop macular degeneration that those who consumed the least amount. The protective carotenoids are found particularly in spinach, kale, and collard greens.

In 1998, Dr. Snodderly and his coworker, Dr. Stewart Richer, went on to suggest an intimate relationship between heart health and eye health—that the two organs share similar nutritional needs. They conclude that "spinach is incredibly important to the eyes." To increase the popularity of spinach, along with diets rich in vegetables and fruits, they feel that physicians might do their patients a service by prescribing cookbooks!

I know these last entries sound a little technical, but I can't help feeling proud that people in my field have finally ventured into preventive medicine.

Good nutrition means following a diet that balances the intake of protein, carbohydrates, fats, vitamins, and minerals (these are all called *nutrients*) against our energy needs, maintenance of a healthy weight, and efficient functioning of our bodies as we journey through life. We're talking here about an easily met challenge if we're willing to try a wide variety of foods, from all the food families: whole grains, legumes, vegetables, fruits, dairy/eggs. It's also important to choose natural products, that is, whole-grain, unprocessed, and without additives. If you can do this, along with the rest of the dietary guidelines, you won't need to worry about taking vitamins or other nutritional supplements, or need to carry a calculator to measure grams of fat versus grams of carbohydrates.

All you have to remember about fat is this one message: *too much fat is harmful.* This concept won't go away soon. In attempting to lower dietary fat intake, the specific emphasis should be on lowering your *saturated fat* intake rather than obsessing about dietary cholesterol. Scientists have determined that only a third of Americans develop an increased blood cholesterol level because of dietary consumption of cholesterol-rich foods. We need to recognize the difference between dietary cholesterol and blood cholesterol. The blood level is apparently related to saturated fats and hydrogenated polyunsaturated fats in the diet. Hydrogenated polyunsaturated fats include animal fats, coconut and palm oil, butter, margarine, and Crisco. Monounsaturated fats, on the other hand, have a beneficial effect on blood cholesterol by lowering the LDL (bad) cholesterol without lowering the HDL (good) cholesterol. This means: *Switch your dietary fat to olive oil and canola oil.*

Remember that eating a variety of plant products (vegetables and grains) will supply you with all the bodily requirements. But a healthy diet doesn't result from just one or two (or three) vegetables. Try for five servings a day. Preparation can be simple. Consider a light steaming, stir-frying in oil (monounsaturated, of course), or adding vegetables to casseroles, soups, pizza, risotto, or pasta.

So what does all this scientific stuff mean for all of us in terms of trying to feed ourselves every day? It means that the style you develop for eating and cooking allows for a lot of individual choices and tastes. In fact, it's essential that you choose a large variety of foods for your personal store of recipes. I hope a lot of them will come from the recipes marked with hearts in this cookbook, but remember, if you exercise regularly, are not badly overweight, and make most of your choices from the healthy list, you should have plenty of room for deviation toward some things that you eat just because you like them. Sweet desserts or simple sugars aren't inherently harmful; they just supply empty calories without providing necessary nutrients.

Now to get back to the original request that started this section. Here are a few nutrient sources to remember as you follow all the dietary guidelines I've set out for you:

Proteins:	grains, milk, legumes (pea and bean family), leafy greens
Fiber:	legumes, fruit
Vitamin A:	carrots, spinach, broccoli, sweet potato, yellow winter squashes, fruit
Vitamin B1 (thiamine):	peas, beans, yeast
Vitamin B2 (riboflavin):	leafy greens, milk
Vitamin B3 (pyridoxine):	spinach, legumes, potatoes, grains, nuts
Vitamin B12:	milk, eggs
Vitamin C:	red, yellow, and green bell peppers, broccoli, tomatoes, fruit (especially citrus)
Vitamin E:	spinach, broccoli, grains, nuts
Calcium:	spinach, kale, broccoli, bok choy, dairy foods, nuts, milk
Caretenoids:	spinach, kale, broccoli, carrots, red bell peppers, sweet potato
Iron:	grains, legumes, eggs, green vegetables

Finally, I want to make a plug for another element of healthy living, namely aerobic exercise. A diet that supplies all the essential nutrients may contain too many calories to be compatible with a sedentary lifestyle (in other words, the pounds will increase if you sit a lot). To increase our metabolic rate in order to use this calorie supply, we need to engage in regular aerobic exercise. Plenty of material has been written about how to do aerobic exercise. I just want to remind you at this point that it's also a necessary ingredient in a healthy lifestyle.

CHAPTER THREE

HORS D'OEUVRES

THIS CHAPTER IS SHORT ON RECIPES because we rarely prepare hors d'oeuvres, literally "dishes outside the meal." When I've worked on a menu for dinner, I don't want anyone spoiling his or her appetite on snacks. I suppose this idea came from my farm background. The cooks worked hard to prepare a hearty meal, whether to feed the working farmers or the extended family at a celebration. There was no need for introductory snacks to "break the ice," nor were there cocktails. The meal was the main thing and the only thing.

Julia tells me that in her Dominican childhood, snacks were served to drop-in guests as a sign that they would not be receiving a meal. You get either a *comida* or hors d'oeuvres but not both. So at our house, hors d'oeuvres are downplayed. I rely on a couple of Vermont cheeses, or an assortment of olives, or a bowl of pistachios in the shell, to keep guests occupied before we get to the dinner table. That way they are not left empty-handed while I excuse myself to go finish cooking in the kitchen.

Two good additions to this short list include Hummus (page 56) served with crackers or small pieces of fresh bread; and Focaccia (page 65).

♥ DEVILED EGGS

At last, eggs have been removed from the "highly restricted" list. This is Grandma Eichner's recipe. She often brings it as an appetizer course, especially good before a summer meal. Pay careful attention to the directions for hard-cooking eggs. Since you'll be aware of the flavor in this recipe, I suggest you look for free-range eggs that are really fresh. When they're just an ingredient in another recipe, it doesn't much matter. But the difference in taste for a fried egg at breakfast or a hard-cooked deviled egg is truly remarkable.

SERVES 6

6 fresh eggs, hard-cooked	½ teaspoon salt
3 tablespoons Mary Murphy's Salad Dressing (see recipe, page 97)	1 to 2 teaspoons Dijon mustard paprika or black pepper, to taste
1 teaspoon white wine vinegar	

OPTIONAL:

chopped anchovies	parsley
chopped smoked salmon	caviar (the caviar was *not*
chopped chives or onions	Grandma Eichner's suggestion.)

To hard-cook the eggs: Place the eggs in a saucepan and cover with cold water. Bring the water to the boiling point, then lower to a simmer and cook 10 minutes (if the eggs start at room temperature; if they come from the refrigerator, add at least 2 minutes more). Immediately remove the eggs from the hot water and bathe in cold water to stop further cooking. (By the way, a soft-cooked egg requires 2 to 3 minutes of simmering after the heat is reduced.)

Peel the eggs carefully, cut in half lengthwise, and remove the yolks with care so as not to damage the whites. Mash the yolks with a fork and moisten them with the salad dressing. (Some people use mayonnaise, but we don't keep it in our house. Julia thinks of it as "American food," something foreign and threatening in her refrigerator.)

Add the vinegar, salt, and mustard. Now place the filling back into the whites, and garnish the top with a dash of paprika or a light dusting of pepper. Serve immediately.

♥ MARINATED MUSHROOMS

This is another recipe from Grandma Eichner, something she started making when she gained a vegetarian daughter-in-law.

SERVES 8

8 to 10 ounces common button-type mushrooms
⅔ cup white wine vinegar
1 medium onion, sliced and separated into rings
1 clove garlic, minced
1 tablespoon sugar
½ teaspoon salt
2 tablespoons water
2 tablespoons olive oil
black pepper, to taste
dash of cayenne

Remove the stems from the mushrooms and discard them. Wash the crowns, pour boiling water over them, and stir for 2 to 3 minutes. Then drain and marinate in the remaining ingredients overnight.

MARY MURPHY'S CHEESE STRAWS

Mary Murphy is a friend from way back. When I came to Middlebury she used her writing talents to inform the world that I had arrived on the scene. Over the years I've had the advantage of sharing many elegant meals that she has hosted. This recipe won't receive any hearts for being heart-healthy, but it's a very tasty and elegant hors d'oeuvre, much easier to make than anyone might imagine.

SERVES 6 TO 8

¼ pound butter (1 stick), at room temperature
3 cups fine, unseasoned breadcrumbs
2 cups shredded sharp Cheddar cheese, lightly packed
1½ cups flour
½ cup milk
½ teaspoon salt
¼ teaspoon Tabasco pepper sauce
dash of paprika
dash of cayenne
Parmesan cheese, grated

Combine all ingredients in a food processor and blend thoroughly. Divide the dough into halves, wrap each half in wax paper, and chill several hours or overnight.

When ready to bake, preheat the oven to 350 degrees F. Roll out one-half of the dough at a time between two layers of wax paper to ⅛-inch thickness. Use a pastry wheel or sharp knife to cut into strips 6 inches long by ½ inch wide, or cut into circles. Sprinkle with Parmesan cheese, spread on a greased baking sheet, and bake until light brown, 10 to 15 minutes.

♥♥♥ ROASTED GARLIC

This treatment of garlic makes a wonderful stand-alone appetizer or you can use it as an ingredient for soups and sauces.

SERVES 4

  2 large, firm heads of garlic (the "head" contains multiple "cloves")

Cut the pointed top of the papery skin off each head of garlic, using a very sharp knife (you may need to use scissors to clip the tops of the cloves extending down from the apex of the head). Go ahead and remove any of the papery cover that comes off easily in your hand, but leave at least one layer of skin on every clove.

Fill a baking pan with ½-inch of water. Place the heads of garlic cut end down in the pan, and bake at 350 degrees for 50 minutes. You can also buy a ceramic garlic roaster in which you can place the prepared garlic heads with just a small amount of olive oil. Either method works fine.

Squeeze the cooked garlic from the remaining skin into a bowl or let your guests do this slightly messy job themselves. Enjoy this special treat on crackers or small pieces of fresh bread.

CHAPTER FOUR

SOUPS

S OUP IS A WONDERFULLY FLEXIBLE food. The cook can "stretch"
soup at the last minute by adding water or a few more key ingredients. It is easy to prepare ahead or freeze for later. There are soups for
starters, soups for main courses, even soups for dessert. Soup can be either vegetarian or meat-based. Soup can be a quick prep by using bouillon cubes, or you can make soup in a slower, purer, fashion using
homemade stock.

I've tried new soup combinations just to use up an overabundance
of garden produce (cucumber, asparagus, lettuce), and have been
pleasantly surprised to find new treasures for our soup list. By the
end of summer we usually have stocked 20 to 30 quarts of soups in
the freezer from various periods of the season's harvest (the time
span marked by a list from asparagus to pumpkin).

And what a pleasure it is in midwinter to heat one of these soups
and smell the aroma of the summer garden, to be reminded that
spring is coming again in a few months.

I've made stocks from animal bones, and stocks from vegetables, but
I prefer the efficiency that comes with good-quality bouillon cubes or
granules. (You may need to adjust for the high salt content in some of
these preparations.) I didn't mind so much simmering the stock pots for
hours "on the back burner" when it was on a wood or coal-fueled cook
stove (heat is a useful by-product in New England winter), but it seems
wasteful on a gas burner. The only stock I make now is Dashi, for flavoring Japanese dishes. Dashi requires only 20 minutes of simmering.

So look at the list of soup recipes. Decide what is in season right now, and plunge in. Make a couple of quarts of soup this weekend that you can sample now and enjoy again later in the week. Remember that you have a lot of latitude with these soup recipes: Vary the seasonings according to your taste, purée or leave chunky, or add a bit of milk or cream when it suits your taste.

♥♥♥ CARROT-GINGER SOUP

I highly recommend this soup because the ingredients for making it are available year-round. It's a quick, very flavorful vegetarian soup.

SERVES 8

2 cloves garlic, chopped fine	1 pound potatoes, peeled
2 large onions (or an equivalent amount of leeks), chopped fine	4 tablespoons fresh gingerroot, chopped
¼ cup olive oil	4 tablespoons fresh parsley, chopped
1 tablespoon red wine vinegar	½ to 1 teaspoon ground cumin
2 pounds carrots, peeled and grated	6 to 7 cups vegetable broth
	salt and black pepper, to taste

Note: If you have a food processor, grate the carrots with the julienne blade, finally cutting the julienne strips into small pieces. Without a processor, simply chop the carrots into matchstick-size pieces. The same process can be used for the potatoes.

Sauté the garlic and onions in ¼ cup of olive oil until tender. Add vinegar and transfer to a stock pot. Add the grated carrots, potatoes, chopped ginger, parsley, spices, and vegetable broth. Bring to a boil and cook until tender (15 to 20 minutes.)

Optional: Purée all or a part. Garnish with chopped parsley or yogurt.

♥♥♥ SPINACH SOUP

Another recipe from Mary Murphy. She makes her version with cream (see below).

SERVES 6

1 medium onion, chopped	6 cups vegetable stock or
4 tablespoons butter	prepared bouillon, heated
1 pound spinach, washed and	salt and black pepper, to taste
chopped coarsely	nutmeg, freshly grated
3 tablespoons flour	

OPTIONAL:

2 gloves garlic, finely chopped
1 tablespoon lemon juice
½-inch piece gingerroot, finely chopped

Sauté the onion in butter (along with garlic, ginger, and lemon juice if you are using them). Add the chopped spinach, and cook over low heat until the spinach is wilted. Sprinkle with flour. Pour in the hot vegetable stock, and stir constantly to bring to a boil. Purée in a processor and return to a saucepan. Season with salt, pepper, and nutmeg.

♥♥ CREAMED SPINACH SOUP

If you desire a richer, creamier soup than the one above, you'll need to drop the number of hearts from 3 to 2. Still not bad considering the nutritional value of spinach.

SERVES 6

same ingredients listed for Spinach Soup, plus:
2 egg yolks
½ cup heavy cream

Follow the directions for Spinach Soup, above. After seasoning the soup, beat the egg yolks with cream, add a little hot soup, then pour the egg-cream mixture back into the soup stirring rapidly. Heat thoroughly but *do not boil*.

♥♥♥ GAZPACHO

I've seen dozens of variations for this chilled summer soup. Many of them call for the addition of onions, cucumbers, and eggs. I've come to like this simple one the best.

SERVES 6

2 to 3	slices stale white French bread, crusts removed	1	cup cold water
6 to 8	very ripe tomatoes, peeled	½	teaspoon ground cumin
3 to 4	cloves garlic	2	tablespoons cilantro leaves, chopped
1	tablespoon olive oil		salt and black pepper, to taste
¼	cup red wine vinegar		

Soak the bread slices in water for 10 minutes, then squeeze out the water. Add the bread to a blender with the rest of the ingredients, and blend until smooth. Adjust seasonings if necessary and chill thoroughly.

Note: This soup will keep several days in the refrigerator.

♥♥♥ TOMATO SOUP (WITH OR WITHOUT LENTILS)

Devised in our kitchen, during the heavy tomato harvest of August of 1995.

SERVES 8

4	shallots, chopped	½	cup red wine
1	large onion, chopped	2	tablespoons balsamic vinegar
4	cloves garlic, chopped		salt and black pepper, to taste
¼	cup olive oil	2 to 4	cups vegetable stock or prepared bouillon (depending on consistency of tomato base)
8 to 10	large tomatoes, chopped		
1	handful fresh basil, chopped		
1	handful fresh parsley, chopped		
1-inch	piece gingerroot, peeled and chopped		

OPTIONAL:

1	cup lentils
½	cup Pesto (see recipe, page 96)
4	ounces Parmesan cheese, grated

Sauté the shallots, garlic, and onion in olive oil in a medium-sized saucepan. Add the tomatoes, herbs, wine, vinegar, salt and pepper, and vegetable stock. Also add the lentils if you choose to do so. Cook for 20 minutes. If you prefer a richer flavor, you may add the pesto at the end. Top with Parmesan cheese.

♥♥♥ KALE SOUP

Here's one to file at the top of the list for nutrition (remember dark leafy greens). A big plus for gardeners is that kale hits peak flavor after frosts, when there is nothing else left in the garden.

SERVES 6

1 large onion, finely chopped
1 clove of garlic, finely chopped
1 tablespoon butter
5 cups vegetable stock
1 pound potatoes, peeled and cubed

¼ teaspoon red pepper flakes
1 large bunch kale, washed,
1 lb. trimmed, and chopped
salt and black pepper, to taste

Sauté the onion and garlic in the butter, in a saucepan large enough for the entire soup. Add the stock, potatoes, and red pepper flakes. Simmer, covered, about 20 minutes, until the potatoes are tender. Blend one-half of the potatoes with a cup of liquid, and add back into saucepan. Steam the kale 5 to 10 minutes, and stir into the soup. Heat and season with salt and pepper.

♥♥♥ WHITE BEAN AND KALE SOUP

I've repeatedly mentioned kale as one of the ultra-healthy green vegetables. Here's another chance to try it in a very flavorful soup that combines greens and high-protein beans.

SERVES 8

3 cups great northern white beans (picked over for stones and dirt, and soaked overnight)
2 large onions, diced
3 cloves garlic, diced
¼ cup olive oil
1 cup carrots, finely diced
½ cup turnips, finely diced

8 cups vegetable stock or prepared bouillon
1 tablespoon fresh basil, chopped
¼ teaspoon red pepper flakes
1 can crushed tomatoes
salt and black pepper, to taste
large bunch of kale, coarsely chopped

Soak the beans overnight, then pour off the soaking water.

Sauté the onions and garlic in the olive oil. Add the carrots and turnips, and continue to sauté until the onions and garlic are tender.

Add all of the above including the beans to a large stockpot. Add the vegetable stock, basil, red pepper flakes, tomatoes, and pepper. Bring all of this to a boil, and skim off any scum that comes to the top of the pot. Simmer for 40 to 50 minutes, until the beans are tender, adding water if needed. Add salt to taste and, finally, a large bunch of coarsely chopped kale. Simmer for another 5 minutes, until the kale is tender.

♥♥♥ PEA SOUP

Here's a soup made from legumes, laden with protein, and low in fat.

SERVES 8

- 1 pound dried split peas
- 2 quarts water
- 2 bouillon cubes
- 1 medium onion, studded with cloves
- 1 teaspoon celery seed
- 2 cloves garlic, crushed
- 1 bay leaf

- 1 teaspoon ground coriander
- 1 teaspoon ground cumin
- ¼ teaspoon red pepper flakes
- ½-inch piece of gingerroot, peeled and chopped
- 2 large carrots, peeled and diced
- salt and black pepper, to taste

OPTIONAL:
- ¼ cup Madeira wine
- 1 cup croutons

Boil the peas in the water with bouillon cubes for 2 minutes, then let set for 1 hour.

Add all other ingredients except wine and croutons, and cook together for about 30 minutes. If desired, add the Madeira at the end of cooking, and top with croutons if you wish.

♥ CHILI

For me, chili is a comfort food from childhood. To be authentic, my chili needs at least a little meat. If vegetarian is your preference, substitute tempeh or cracked wheat.

SERVES 6

- 3 cups dried red beans (kidney, pinto, or cranberry beans), soaked overnight (the water level in the pot should be twice the height of the beans)
- 1 pound lean ground beef (chuck or round)
- 2 medium onions, chopped coarsely
- 4 cloves of garlic, chopped fine
- ¼ cup olive oil
- 3 tablespoons flour
- ½ teaspoon ground cumin

- ½ to 1 teaspoon ground coriander
- ¼ teaspoon chili powder
- ¼ teaspoon red pepper flakes
- ½ teaspoon dried oregano
- ½ teaspoon dried basil
- chopped green chilies (sweet or hot depending on your taste)
- 6 to 8 large fresh tomatoes, chopped (or 1 large can cooked tomatoes or 1 quart Marinara Sauce; see recipe, page 94)
- salt and black pepper, to taste

After soaking the beans overnight, drain off the water and replace with fresh. Cook until tender, about 40 minutes.

Meanwhile, prepare the ground beef by browning—cooking quickly over high heat to achieve a brown color with a moist interior—in a skillet with onions and garlic in olive oil, while sprinkling with 3 tablespoons of flour. Add salt and pepper to taste. Mix in the cumin, coriander, chili powder, red pepper flakes, oregano, basil, and green chilies. Then add tomatoes (or marinara) and simmer the entire mixture for 1 to 2 hours as needed to reach the desired consistency and to deepen the flavor. Add more water or marinara sauce as needed. Add the chopped parsley at the very end.

Note: Chili can be frozen and reheated later.

TOMATOES IN SEASON

Many of my older patients who give up gardening due to physical disability or space limitation continue to raise one or two tomato plants, even if in a pot on the front step. The tomato is every New England gardener's favorite crop, probably because we fantasize about that perfect red jewel from mid-October until the beginning of August again the next year. Our precious fresh tomato season is about six weeks long, perhaps eight if we have a really lucky year.

How then to best utilize the abundance, from the first ripe specimen in early August through the buckets of late-season fruits spilling off the kitchen counter when the first killing frost arrives in September or October? Any gardener will tell you that the very best way to enjoy a tomato is in the garden, around midday, when the sun is hot. Pick the reddest tomato you can find, hold it by the stem, and chomp away until you're left with the stem in your hand, juice all over your face, and your mouth filled with the most wonderful tomato flavor you can imagine.

A slightly more civilized approach would be to bring in the tomatoes directly from the garden for lunch or dinner, slice them, then drizzle them with extra-virgin olive oil, and sprinkle them with a few grains of course salt, freshly ground black pepper, and chopped fresh basil leaves. Incidentally, a large plate of these is an excellent addition to a summer potluck supper.

For a first course, try slices or wedges of ripe tomatoes combined with either fresh or aged goat cheese, or fresh mozzarella. The flavors of tomato and cheese seem made for each other. Another method is to halve a tomato, sprinkle the top with Parmesan, and broil it until the cheese is melted and the tomato is hot and tender.

My favorite pasta sauce can only be made during the six-week period of fresh tomato season. It's simple—just chop the fresh, very ripe tomatoes coarsely, peels and all, and add to a pan in which you've sautéed minced garlic and olive oil.

A few tips about the handling of tomatoes:

1. They're best sliced with a sharp, serrated knife.
2. There is no better way to kill a fresh tomato than to put it in the refrigerator.
3. If you ever need to peel a tomato for a recipe, lower it into boiling water for 30 to 60 seconds, then pull it out and rinse it under cold water. The peel will slip off in your hand.

♥♥♥ PUMPKIN-GARLIC SOUP

This recipe came from a mailing from the Middlebury Natural Foods Co-op. It's absolutely delicious.

SERVES 8

2 large onions or 4 leeks (white and yellow portion only), chopped fine
4 ounces butter or ¼ cup olive oil
2 heads of garlic
2 teaspoons ground allspice
1 tablespoon ground coriander

4 cups pumpkin, baked and diced (or canned if you prefer)
4 cups vegetable or chicken stock (or more if needed for desired consistency)
1 cup dry sherry or dry white wine

OPTIONAL:

4 teaspoons fresh cilantro, chopped
4 teaspoons pumpkin seeds, roasted

To prepare pumpkin, use a heavy knife to cut into four or more pieces. Clean the seeds and seed matrix from the flesh. Bake the pumpkin pieces in a shallow pan containing 1 inch of water, for 20 to 30 minutes at 350 degrees F until tender. Then dice or purée as needed.

Roast the two heads of garlic (see recipe, page 26)

Meanwhile, sauté the onions or leeks (or a combination thereof) in oil or butter.

When the garlic is roasted, squeeze the cooked garlic from the remaining skin into a stockpot. Add the onions, spices, pumpkin, stock, and wine. Bring to a simmer, and heat gently for 20 minutes to combine the flavors. Stir occasionally. Top with chopped cilantro leaves or roasted pumpkin seeds.

♥ ONION SOUP AU GRATIN

This recipe is simple in terms of ingredients, a bit time-consuming, but fantastically good.

SERVES 6

4 large onions, thinly sliced	2 tablespoons port wine
½ stick butter	6 slices French bread, toasted
¼ cup minus 1 teaspoon sugar	4 ounces Gruyère cheese, grated
6 cups vegetable stock	salt and black pepper, to taste

Cook the onions in butter in a medium-sized saucepan over medium-low heat, covered, for 20 minutes, stirring occasionally. Sprinkle the sugar over the onions, toss, and cook uncovered until they become golden brown, about 10 minutes. Add the salt and pepper.

Add 3 cups of stock, and simmer uncovered for 15 minutes. Add the remaining 3 cups of stock and port wine. Cook another 30 to 40 minutes.

Divide the soup into six oven-proof bowls, topping each with French bread. Sprinkle the cheese atop the toast. Broil or bake until the cheese melts and the soup is bubbly.

♥♥♥ LEEK AND POTATO SOUP

This is a jewel. It tastes great, is always a crowd-pleaser, and stores easily in the freezer. The only problem might be to obtain the leeks (try growing them yourself). Potatoes, on the other hand, are always available. Since for me they come from the garden, I'm reminded of when my daughters were young children, picking up the potatoes after I dug them. As laborers go, they were very reasonable; I paid them 25 cents per bucket.

SERVES 8

6 to 8 medium to large leeks, sliced (use the white part along with the yellow transition area, but not the green tops)	6 cups vegetable stock
	1½ teaspoons salt
	½ teaspoon grated nutmeg
	¼ teaspoon ground mace
4 tablespoons butter	
2 pounds potatoes, peeled and diced	

OPTIONAL:

1 cup heavy cream
handful of chives, parsley, or watercress, chopped
diced celeriac (celery root) to substitute for part of the potatoes

Note: You can process the leeks gently with the metal blade in a food processor, but be careful not to liquefy them.

Sauté the leeks in the butter in a stockpot. Add the potatoes and vegetable stock. Bring to a boil, and simmer until tender, about 15 minutes. Add the salt, nutmeg, and mace.

You may purée all or a portion of the soup. We like ours in the more granular form. Add cream, if desired, after the puréeing, while reheating. This is also the point at which you may add chives, parsley, or watercress for a touch of green.

Note: This soup can be frozen and reheated later.

♥♥♥ LEEK-TOMATO-CARROT SOUP

Yet another way to use a lot of the leek harvest when it comes in late summer or early fall. This soup freezes nicely for winter.

SERVES 8

6 to 8 medium leeks (use white and yellow portion only), finely chopped

2 pounds carrots, peeled and grated

4 cloves garlic, finely chopped

2 to 4 cups vegetable stock (I use bouillon cubes)

4 cups Marinara Sauce (see recipe, page 94)

4 tablespoons butter (or substitute ¼ cup olive oil)

salt and black pepper, to taste

Sauté leeks and garlic in butter or olive oil until tender. Combine with the carrots and marinara sauce, and cook until all ingredients are tender, about 10 minutes. Add stock for desired consistency.

LEEKS

Leeks are the most regal of the vegetables I grow. Their culture spans the length of my Vermont garden season: I plant the seeds indoors in early February, a full month before the tomato seeds, and we're still bringing leeks in from the garden in the winter until I have to chop the surrounding frozen soil with an axe. Looking down each morning from the bedroom window at the two straight rows, I see the leeks as the most elegant and formal entry in my vegetable collection.

I set out the young seedlings when I suspect we're through with hard frosts in the early spring. I drop them into deep slender holes at the bottom of a trench. As they grow, I gradually pull in the sides of the trench so that, eventually, 6 inches of the plant is below the soil level. This is my method of "blanching" the leeks in order to elongate the white part. We start our leek harvest in midsummer, when they are only half an inch in diameter, by "thinning out" every other plant. Those that remain grow into the one-inch beauties that we harvest when the weather gets cold.

The leek is a close relative of the onion, but its milder flavor makes it a versatile ingredient for soups, casseroles, and pies. When the final harvest comes in, we chop some leeks and freeze them in plastic bags to use in cooking through the winter.

♥♥ MUSHROOM AND WILD RICE SOUP

This is a great recipe for winter when there might be a shortage of fresh produce. It has a rich mushroom flavor and is definitely low in fat.

SERVES 6

1 medium onion, finely chopped	4 to 6 ounces each of three kinds of fresh dark mushrooms (shitaki, oyster, etc.) or 1 ounce each if dry
1 tablespoon butter	
⅓ cup wild rice	
6 to 7 cups vegetable stock (or prepared bouillon)	1 carrot, peeled and cut into matchstick-size strips
4 cloves garlic, chopped	salt and black pepper, to taste

Sauté the onion and wild rice for 2 minutes in the butter in a medium-sized saucepan. Stir in the vegetable stock. Cover and simmer for 25 minutes, stirring occasionally. Add the chopped garlic, cover, and simmer another 15 minutes, until the rice is almost tender. Add the mushrooms. Simmer, covered, for another 10 minutes. Preparation to this point can be done one day ahead and refrigerated.

Just before serving, stir the carrot strips into the soup, and simmer for 2 minutes until the carrots are crisp and tender. Season with salt and pepper.

MUSHROOMS

For anyone who avoids meat, mushrooms make a great stand-in. Consider their dark color (like well-done pot roast), earthy aroma, and intense meaty flavor. A properly grilled Portabello will (almost) hold up against a broiled filet mignon in terms of tender chewiness, hearty flavor, and rich brown color. Then there's the big plus: no cholesterol, no saturated fat, and almost no calories. Of course, mushrooms contain almost no nutrients either, but then, with such a flavorful gift from the forest floor, who can complain?

I'm talking, of course, about wild mushrooms. The common "button" type, long grown commercially, are bland in comparison. Fortunately, today, you can avail yourself of wild mushrooms without the bother or risk of hunting them yourself. Specialty food stores (including our natural food co-op) carry two or three types throughout most of the year, thanks to professional hunters and growers.

Some of my favorite recipes in this book owe their tastiness and texture to mushrooms: soup, risotto, and spinach stir-fry. We often rely on dried mushrooms for at least a major portion of the mushrooms in a recipe. Reconstituting dried mushrooms restores their flavor and texture: simply cover with hot broth or boiling water and set them aside for 20 to 30 minutes before using.

My wife is such a big fan of mushrooms that I once gave her a growing kit (for oyster mushrooms and morels). That was not one of my do-it-yourself successes. The kit came with impressive instructions and packaging, but the mushrooms never materialized. Fortunately, she admires me more for my cooking than my gift choices.

CHAPTER FIVE

VEGETABLES

"EAT YOUR VEGETABLES!" Sounds like punishment. For some of us it was when we were growing up, especially if vegetables meant the same two or three varieties, overcooked, faded in color, or mashed with a pasty cream sauce. This isn't my history, but I've eaten in enough school cafeterias, military mess lines, and bad diners to know what bad vegetables are all about.

I've read that some big-time chefs loathe serving vegetarians in their restaurants because the vegetarians find the offerings limited in number or creativity. Personally, I am grateful to my vegetarian wife for teaching me how easy it is to add vegetables to our menu, and how important is their selection. I've come to appreciate how vegetables can punctuate a meal by their color or flavor.

I'm grateful for a sojourn I made to southern India, where I learned how diverse a vegetarian cuisine can be. Diverse not only in variety of vegetables, grains, and legumes, but also in the many herbs and spices that can be used to vary the flavor and presentation of the basic ingredients. I finally gave up the idea that a good soup or casserole had to have a meat stock in order to be flavorful.

Thanks also to George Bush, who convinced me that it is okay to not like broccoli. That leaves more space in my garden for the other eighteen or twenty vegetables that I love so much.

Hating vegetables just won't do if you are going to develop a nutritious food-style. One look at the food pyramid tells us that plant foods—vegetables and fruits, along with grains—make the basis for healthy eating. Don't despair if you can't stand kohlrabi. It doesn't matter if you hate any vegetable that is red. There are plenty of colors to choose from.

However, if you are going to eat the recommended three to five servings of vegetables daily, you may have to broaden your thinking. Learn how to buy or grow vegetables so that you will carry high quality into your kitchen.

Having your own garden may allow you the most choices and the ultimate in freshness. You can enjoy plants bred for eating rather than cross-country travel. Of course, you also save money on the vegetables you grow yourself, plus you receive the free benefit of the exercise you get in the process.

To our delight, we've even been able to (slowly) convince our neighbor farmers in the Dominican Republic that eating vegetables along with their rice and beans can be a savory treat, even if they don't understand our admonitions about nutritional requirements. It helps in the argument to be able to show them that they can grow these products in their own gardens rather than paying for them.

When you bring your well-chosen vegetables into the kitchen (from the garden, farmers' market, food co-op, or natural food store), be careful how you store and handle them. If possible, shop or harvest frequently to avoid long storage. When you must store, keep spinach, lettuce, broccoli, and peppers in the refrigerator. Potatoes belong in a dark, cool, spot outside the refrigerator. Tomatoes and fruits lose flavor if refrigerated. Onions, pumpkins, and winter squash store well in a dry and slightly cool location.

I remember, growing up on a farm, having a root cellar for storing potatoes, carrots, beans, onions, and other crops for winter use. You may find a cool, dry space in your basement or pantry to store some of these items from a bountiful harvest.

Canning and freezing are two preservation methods I learned from my Nebraska childhood. I'm not a fan of frozen corn or green beans as such, but we use our freezer to store many quarts of soup and ratatouille, prepared when the ingredients are fresh from the garden.

Canning was an art practiced in every farm kitchen before the days of freezers. I remember the gleaming jars of vegetables and fruits that filled the basement shelves at the end of every growing season. However, I don't remember that the flavor of these vegetables quite matched up to their appearance in the jars. The steam pressure cooking required for safe preservation was not only a cumbersome process but it significantly altered both the texture and the flavor of the vegetables.

Yet I haven't completely discarded the concept of canning. I use it to preserve tomatoes (as Marinara Sauce; see page 94) and French green beans (in a dilled vinegar brine.) However, I do not use a pressure steamer. The acidity of the tomatoes and the pickled green beans allows for safe preservation by using the boiling water bath instead.

The third thing you can do to shift your impression of vegetables from "punishment" to "reward" is to learn to prepare them so that you can preserve or enhance their natural flavor. Don't just boil them into submission so that all the goodness (taste and nutrients) is given up to water that you pour down the drain. Invest in a steamer, either a metal basket to fit into a saucepan or a bamboo steamer to set over a small amount of water in a wok. Wash the vegetables, trim off blemishes or tough parts, and steam them over an inch of water for the shortest time needed to tenderize them. Start at 4 minutes for a trial and increase by 1-minute increments if needed. Serve immediately with a squeeze of lemon juice.

Some vegetables will taste better with stir-frying, using a small amount of olive, canola, or peanut oil in a wok or heavy frying pan over high heat. Again, keep the time short—2 to 4 minutes—and add just a dash of lemon juice or soy sauce before serving. (We use natural *shoyu*—fermented from soybeans and cracked wheat—rather than the several Chinese brands of soy sauce available in supermarkets, which are prepared from hydrolyzed vegetable proteins. *Tamari* is a progenitor of shoyu, made without wheat.)

With time, experience, and experimentation, you will find enjoyable ways to combine vegetables, to dress them up with sauces, and to use them as ingredients in more complex dishes. I am hoping that you will get the surprise that I did—vegetables are great. Whether served as a side dish, a soup, or a main course, vegetables can be the basis of a meal. Even some chefs are learning from the vegetarians, so you may as well join the crowd if you are serious about eating healthfully.

♥ SPINACH CASSEROLE

This recipe is from my old friend Diane Neuse. I asked her for some vegetarian recipes when I started cooking for the woman who eventually became my partner.

SERVES 6 TO 8

1	medium onion, chopped	⅛	teaspoon nutmeg, grated
2	cloves garlic, chopped	½	cup Parmesan cheese, grated
¼	cup butter	½	cup dry unseasoned bread
12 to 16	ounces fresh spinach,		crumbs
	washed		salt and black pepper, to taste
¾	cup cream	¼	cup Cheddar cheese, grated
¾	cup whole milk		

Sauté the onion and garlic in the butter. Steam the spinach for 4 to 5 minutes, then chop with a sharp knife. Mix the sautéed onions and garlic with the cream, milk, nutmeg, Parmesan cheese, bread crumbs, salt, and pepper.

Place all of the above into a greased 9-by-9-inch baking dish, and top with the Cheddar cheese. Bake for 30 minutes at 350 degrees F.

Note: This becomes a three-heart recipe if you substitute olive oil for the butter, nonfat yogurt for the cream, and skim milk for whole milk.

♥♥♥ SPINACH AND PORTABELLO MUSHROOM STIR-FRY

Cooking for a vegetarian, I'm always searching for quick recipes that will provide some diversity. Also, I'm ever more convinced that leafy greens (spinach and kale being at the top of the list) are important as antioxidants in our diet. Perhaps they really can prevent diseases such as macular degeneration and hardening of the arteries. So I'm always looking for ways to present the vegetable that I happen to love—spinach.

SERVES 6

1	large bunch (12 to 16 ounces) fresh spinach	1	teaspoon toasted sesame oil
		½	teaspoon soy sauce
2	Portabello mushrooms	2 to 3	tablespoons olive oil
	juice of one lemon (or two to three tablespoons)	2	cloves garlic, minced
		½	tablespoon fresh ginger root,
1	teaspoon fish sauce (sometimes we stretch "vegetarian" when it comes to fish)		minced

Wash and coarsely chop the spinach. Cut the stems from the mushrooms, and with a towel, brush any dirt from the outer surface of the mushrooms. Slice the mushroom cap into strips ½-inch wide, and cut them to a length of no more than 2 inches.

Mix the lemon juice, fish sauce, sesame oil, and soy sauce.

Drizzle the olive oil into a hot wok, add the garlic and ginger, and fry for approximately 1 minute, until the garlic begins to brown.

Add the mushrooms, and cook for 1 minute. Add the spinach, and stir-fry until wilted and tender. Add the sauce mixture for a final 15 seconds of stir-frying.

♥ GREEN PEPPER VEGETABLE AU GRATIN

The French phrase au gratin *typically means sliced or chopped vegetables layered in a baking dish covered with a sauce and baked until a brown crust forms. The many wonderful variations use summer vegetables, fall root vegetables, or potatoes, with or without cheese, cream, buttermilk, or breadcrumbs. By all means do scrape the crispy parts from the dish. Think of a gratin as either a side dish or a main course.*
We devised this one, with some help from our friend Judy Yarnall, in the summer of 1996, when we had a particularly heavy crop of green peppers.

SERVES 8 TO 10

¼ cup olive oil	2 to 3 cloves of garlic, crushed
salt and black pepper, to taste	4 eggs
1 teaspoon ground cumin	1½ cups yogurt or buttermilk
1 teaspoon ground coriander	1½ cups Gruyère cheese, grated
1 teaspoon dried mustard	½ cup dry unseasoned
3 to 4 leeks, sliced in thin rounds	breadcrumbs
4 to 5 small zucchini and summer squash	¼ to ½ cup Parmesan cheese, grated
6 green peppers, cut into thin strips	

Prepare a dressing consisting of the olive oil, salt and black pepper, cumin, coriander, and mustard. Then toss the prepared vegetables in a bowl with this dressing. Beat together the eggs and yogurt or buttermilk.

Layer as follows in an oiled 9-by-12-inch baking dish: first half the vegetables, then a layer of cheese; repeat with another layer of vegetables and a final layer of cheese. Then pour the egg mixture over everything, and top with breadcrumbs and grated Parmesan cheese. Bake for 30 to 40 minutes at 375 degrees F, until the contents are bubbling and the top is a nice crispy brown.

♥ GERMAN POTATO SALAD

You may wonder, with an author named Eichner, why you'll find so few references to German food in this cookbook. I have in fact traveled extensively in Germany, seeking out my ancestral roots. I admire a lot of things about Germany and Germans, but cuisine is not one of them. True, the fancy dessert pastries, delectable sausages, and fine lagers are all very tempting, but how can you make these the basis for a healthy diet? For me, German cuisine is the antithesis of what I'm trying to promote in this book. However, I include the following recipe because, except for the bacon, it is low-fat and an excellent way to utilize potatoes during their season.

SERVES 8

2½ pounds potatoes, peeled and cut into 1-inch slices	2 tablespoons sugar
8 slices bacon	1½ teaspoons salt
½ cup cider vinegar	¼ teaspoon black pepper
2 tablespoons cornstarch	1 teaspoon celery seed

OPTIONAL:

    1 tablespoon green onion, chopped

Cook the potatoes in salted water to cover until just done. Drain and allow to cool, then dice to ½-inch pieces.

Fry the bacon, then remove from the pan and discard most of the grease. Add 1 cup of water to the pan, heat, and stir to loosen the brown bits.

Add the vinegar, cornstarch, sugar, salt, pepper, and celery seed. Simmer, stirring until the sauce is blended and thickened. Pour the sauce over the cooked potatoes and serve at room temperature. The salad may be garnished with chopped green onion.

♥ MASHED POTATOES

When I was growing up, we had potatoes at least once every day. For holidays and special meals, they were mashed. So for me this extra touch elevates everyday food into the category of celebratory food. The following recipe should be enough for six people if they're not farmers at hard labor.

SERVES 6

2 pounds potatoes, washed, peeled, and cubed (I like Yukon Gold the best)	4 to 8 tablespoons butter salt and black pepper, to taste
½ to 1 cup milk	

Place the potatoes in a large saucepan, cover with cold water, and bring to a boil. Simmer until tender to the pierce of a fork, anywhere from 12 to 20 minutes depending on the age of the potatoes.

While the potatoes are cooking, heat the milk. When the potatoes are done, drain them, and place in a large mixing bowl. Begin mashing with either a heavy-duty mixer or a potato masher. Add hot milk to desired consistency, butter, and salt and pepper to taste. Continue beating until smooth, unless you prefer that your mashed potatoes have an occasional lump, for character.

Mashed potatoes should be served hot, thus the reason for preheating the milk, and for working fast through the process. This can be a bit of a challenge if it's part of getting a whole Thanksgiving dinner on the table while everything is hot.

Two variations include the substitution of celeriac (celery root) for one-third of the potatoes, or the addition of two cloves of garlic to the potatoes before you begin boiling (whip them right along with the potatoes). Or, add a few cloves of Roasted Garlic just before mashing (see recipe, page 26).

Note: "Potato water" saved from boiling the potatoes can be used to add flavor to gravy.

POTATOES DAUPHINOISE

This is another recipe that Julia learned from her sister Tita. This method of preparing potatoes may not be low-fat, but it's sure to please everyone's taste. We think of it as quite rich, but when we once served it to a young woman from Provence, she was surprised that we didn't make it with more heavy cream.

SERVES 8 TO 10

2 pounds Yukon Gold potatoes, cleaned and sliced thin

6 ounces Gruyère cheese, grated

1 medium onion, chopped

grated nutmeg

1 cup heavy cream

Layer one-half of the potatoes in the bottom of a greased 9-by-12-inch baking dish, and sprinkle with onion. Layer with one-half of the cheese. Then add a second layer of potatoes, with salt and pepper to taste, and a dusting of grated nutmeg. Add the heavy cream and the final layer of cheese. Bake at 400 degrees F for 30 minutes, covered with foil. Then uncover, and bake for another 30 minutes, until brown on top.

Note: Substitute low-fat milk or yogurt for a portion of the heavy cream to reduce the fat.

♥♥♥ OVEN-ROASTED SUMMER VEGETABLES

We enjoy lots of ways of preparing and eating the multitude of summer vegetables that we bring in from the garden. This has come to be our favorite. Originally, I tried grilling the same vegetables over an open fire, but a friend, Alastair Reid, dubbed the recipe, "Bill's burnt vegetables." Therefore, I was happy to learn of this oven-roasted method, suggested by Julia's sister Maury. Besides eliminating the occasional charred taste, it's also much easier because the small pieces don't fall into the open fire.

SERVES 8

¾	cup olive oil	3	medium onions, preferably the red variety, quartered and separated
4	cloves garlic, minced		
2	teaspoons fresh oregano, chopped	2	large red bell peppers, sliced
¼	cup fresh basil, chopped	3 to 4	zucchini, sliced
2	teaspoons balsamic vinegar salt and black pepper, to taste	8 to 10	Roma tomatoes, halved or quartered
2	large or 6 to 8 small eggplants		

Note: If the eggplant are large, you will need to peel, slice, and prebake them for 10 minutes at 375 degrees F. If you are using the small, thin, Japanese variety, they can be sliced, and peeled, and added to the rest of the vegetables without baking.

Prepare a dressing by mixing the olive oil, garlic, oregano, basil, vinegar, salt, and pepper. Add the dressing to the prepared vegetables, and stir until well mixed. Spread the vegetables onto one or two oven sheets and roast at 400 degrees F for 20 minutes, or until tender. Watch for browning, in which case some of the vegetables may need to be stirred or turned. Serve warm or at room temperature.

♥ VEGETABLE CASSEROLE

This hearty one-dish recipe works well as a vegetable side dish or a main course for lunch or a light supper. Just add whole-grain bread and a salad.

SERVES 8 TO 10

2 medium/large eggplants, sliced

2 medium onions, sliced thin

1 leek, sliced thin

3 cloves garlic, chopped

4 tablespoons olive oil

black pepper, to taste

2 to 3 small zucchini, sliced

1 red bell pepper, cut into strips

1 green bell pepper, cut into strips

1 cube vegetable bouillon

6 Roma tomatoes, chopped

¼ cup cilantro, chopped

¼ cup fresh parsley, chopped

4 tablespoons basil leaves, shredded

1 tablespoon fresh oregano, chopped

½ teaspoon ground cumin

salt, to taste

1 cup Gruyère cheese, grated

3 tablespoons Parmesan cheese, grated

Bake the eggplant slices for 15 minutes at 400 degrees F on an oiled oven sheet, let cool, then cube.

Sauté the onions, leek, and garlic in olive oil until tender. Add black pepper. Stir-fry the zucchini and bell peppers. Add the cube of vegetable bouillon.

Combine all of the above in a large saucepan. Add the chopped tomatoes, and cook briefly. Add the herbs and salt, then layer all of the above in a 9-by-12-inch baking dish, topped with the grated cheeses. Bake at 375 degrees F for 30 minutes.

♥♥♥ RATATOUILLE

After trying many recipes, I finally landed on this modification. Another dish to celebrate the late-summer vegetable harvest.

SERVES 8

1 or 2	large eggplants, cut lengthwise into thick slices	salt and black pepper, to taste
3	medium onions, sliced	2 bay leaves
6	cloves garlic, chopped	1 tablespoon fresh oregano, chopped
⅓	cup olive oil	1 tablespoon fresh thyme, chopped
1½	red bell peppers, cut into wide strips	1 pound or more zucchini, thickly sliced
1½	green bell peppers, cut into wide strips	4 tablespoons fresh basil leaves, chopped
1½	pounds or more ripe tomatoes, peeled or unpeeled and cut into wedges or large chunks	

Place the eggplant slices cut side down on an oiled baking sheet. Bake at 450 degrees F for 15 minutes. Remove from the heat, let cool, and dice.

Sauté the sliced onions and one-half the garlic in one-half of the olive oil. Then add additional olive oil as needed, the diced eggplant, and the red and green peppers. Cook over low heat for about 10 minutes, stirring frequently. Add 1 pound of the tomatoes, the remaining garlic, salt, black pepper, bay leaves, oregano, and thyme. Continue cooking over low heat, stirring regularly, until the vegetables are almost submerged in their own liquid. Then bring the heat to high. Boil these juices for a moment, stirring, then lower the heat, cover partially, and simmer for an hour, stirring occasionally. Finally, add the zucchini, the remaining tomatoes, and the basil leaves. Simmer for another 20 to 30 minutes, until the zucchini is just tender but still colorful. Serve warm.

♥♥♥ WILD RICE RATATOUILLE

This is a nice combination of a grain and vegetables. The cooking process is much quicker than for the standard ratatouille.

SERVES 6

⅔ cup wild rice
2 cups water
1 medium onion, sliced
3 cloves garlic, chopped
3 tablespoons olive oil
salt and black pepper, to taste
3 small zucchini, sliced
2 green bell peppers, cut into strips

1 red bell pepper, cut in strips
1 medium eggplant
8 plum tomatoes, diced
1 teaspoon fresh oregano, chopped
2 tablespoons fresh, basil leaves, chopped
1 to 2 cups Marinara Sauce (see recipe, page 94)

Cook the rice in boiling water, covered, for 50 minutes or until tender, stirring occasionally.

Sauté the onion and garlic in olive oil until tender. Add salt and black pepper. Set aside.

Stir-fry the zucchini and bell peppers. Peel and slice the eggplant, bake for 10 minutes at 375 degrees F, and then stir-fry.

Combine all the ingredients, including the cooked rice. Add marinara as needed for consistency. Cook briefly to mix the flavors.

♥♥♥ LEEK AND CARROT SAUTÉ

A great way to combine two late-season garden crops.

SERVES 6 TO 8 (AS A SIDE DISH)

3 cloves garlic, chopped
3 leeks, sliced
3 tablespoons butter or olive oil
2 pounds carrots, sliced

salt and black pepper, to taste
1 teaspoon ground cumin
chopped parsley (for garnish)

Sauté the garlic and leeks in the butter or olive oil. Add the sliced carrots, salt, pepper, and cumin. Simmer the mixture, covered, for 5 to 8 minutes. Garnish with the parsley.

♥♥♥ LEEKS AND SUNDRIED TOMATOES

Another way to enjoy the elegant leek. If you happen to make this early enough in the fall so that they're still available, fresh tomatoes can be substituted for the sundried ones.

SERVES 6 TO 8 (AS A SIDE DISH)

3 to 4 leeks, sliced
    2 tablespoons olive oil
    2 tablespoons red wine vinegar
    2 cloves garlic, minced
   ½ cup sundried tomatoes, chopped (the oil-packed variety)

2 tablespoons fresh basil, chopped
salt and black pepper, to taste
1 tablespoon water

Sauté the leeks in the olive oil until tender. Add vinegar, garlic, tomatoes, basil, salt, pepper, and water. Cook, covered, for another 15 minutes. Serve hot or at room temperature.

"SUNDRIED" TOMATOES

Drying, or dehydrating, tomatoes concentrates the flavor, color, and sweetness of the ripe summer fruit into a chewy condiment that keeps indefinitely for off-season use. In fact, in any season, a few strips on a pizza or in a salad or pasta sauce will add a distinctive tomato flavor more pungent than is possible with a fresh tomato.

Sundried tomatoes are available in two forms: packed in olive oil or packaged dry in airtight containers. The dried type is best reconstituted with oil or water before use. Either type tends to be expensive. In fact, I always thought of sundried tomatoes as a luxury that only those who might have caviar and champagne for breakfast would stock in their pantries. Certainly the summer climate is not dependably dry enough here in Vermont that I could dry my excess home-grown tomatoes myself.

But then somebody suggested "sun-drying" them in the oven, and it worked! When I've accumulated a good supply of really ripe Italian plum tomatoes (really the only type that dries well) I wash them, remove the stems, and cut them in half (the long way) in butterfly fashion. I place them cut-side up on oven trays wiped with olive oil, and keep them in the oven at a very low temperature (150 degrees F) overnight. (This makes a good weekend project because you need to be available to remove them at different times the next morning—some are "done" sooner than others.) Then I pack them in small jars, layering in fresh basil leaves and a couple of garlic cloves, and covering the whole batch with olive oil. I cover the jars tightly and store in a cool place.

This way I can enjoy a luxury that doesn't cost much after all, and save my pennies for buying champagne and caviar.

♥♥♥ CARROTS VICHY

This is an extremely simple and quick recipe when your menu calls for one more vegetable side dish, and is appropriate at any time of the year.

SERVES 6 TO 8

1½ pounds carrots, peeled and
 cut into very thin rounds
salt and black pepper, to taste

1 teaspoon sugar
¼ cup water
4 tablespoons butter

OPTIONAL:

1 tablespoon parsley, chopped
1 teaspoon gingerroot, chopped

Place all the ingredients into a skillet. Cover with a round of wax paper and cook over moderately high heat, shaking the skillet occasionally, for about 10 minutes. You're finished when the carrots are tender and lightly glazed, and the liquid has disappeared. Take care not to let the carrots burn or dry out. Serve sprinkled with chopped parsley or a bit of chopped ginger.

♥♥♥ SWEET-AND-SOUR CARROTS

We call these zanahorias agridulce, *because this is a recipe from Tía Rosa in the Dominican Republic. She found this a tasty offering for her vegetarian niece (Julia) when she visited from the United States. We found the original recipe much too sweet, so we've reduced the sugar to one-half cup (or even less if you prefer).*

SERVES 8

- 2 pounds carrots, peeled and sliced
- 3 medium onions, coarsely chopped
- 3 green or red bell peppers, cut into narrow strips
- ¾ cup cider vinegar
- ½ cup sugar
- ½ cup canola oil
- 1 cup of canned tomato soup (or Marinara Sauce; see recipe, page 94)
- 1 teaspoon dried mustard
- 1 teaspoon Worcestershire sauce

Cook the carrots in boiling water until just tender. Remove, rinse in cold water, and cut into thick rounds. Set aside.

Steam the chopped onions and bell peppers (separately) until just tender, each about 2 minutes.

Heat the cider vinegar with sugar until the sugar is completely dissolved. Add the canola oil, tomato soup, mustard, and Worcestershire sauce. Mix thoroughly, then add the sauce to the carrots, peppers, and onions. Serve at room temperature as a side dish.

♥♥ BUTTERNUT SQUASH AU GRATIN

The apples and spices add extra zest to this fall casserole.

SERVES 8 (IF USED AS A SIDE DISH)

- 3 tablespoons olive oil
- 2 medium onions, chopped
- 3 cloves garlic, minced
- 2 apples, peeled, cored, and chopped
- 1 butternut squash, peeled and cubed
- ½ stick butter, melted
- 1 cup vegetable stock
- 1 teaspoon fresh gingerroot, chopped
- ½ teaspoon ground cumin
- ⅓ cup Gruyère cheese, grated
- 4 tablespoons dry unseasoned breadcrumbs
- salt and black pepper, to taste

Sauté the onions and garlic in the olive oil. Mix with the apples, squash, butter, stock, and spices. Place the mixture in a 9-by-9-inch oiled baking dish. Top with the grated cheese and breadcrumbs. Bake for 30 minutes at 375 degrees F.

CHAPTER SIX

GRAINS AND LEGUMES

L OOK AT THE FOOD GUIDE PYRAMID (see page 16). You'll see that grains represent the ground floor of the diet you should aspire to. Consider bread, the "staff of life"; or rice eaten three times a day by half the world's population; corn tortillas, which are a staple south of our border; or pasta, the "first plate" in a major cuisine of the world. For much of the world, grains are the most important food. The population groups for whom that is true were the first ones studied by our scientists in order to learn why they have such a low incidence of the diseases that are killing us here in the "developed world": heart disease, diabetes, and cancer.

Combine grains with their cousins the legumes, and you have a nearly perfect combination of proteins, complex carbohydrates, and monounsaturated fats, plus a high fiber content. Learn to eat a variety of beans and whole grains (try to avoid the refined versions) and you'll meet your requirement for vitamins and minerals (micronutrients) as well.

I learned the words to the song, "America," in the first grade of my one-room country school. Living in the midst of "amber waves of grain" and working on the "fruited plains," I came to learn why that area was called the breadbasket of our nation. But I only knew that the amber-colored wheat and the high-yield corn and soybeans were used as animal feed. Everything we harvested was processed, then laced with hormones and antibiotics, and fed to the beef cattle, hogs, and lambs on neighboring farms. The only Midwest farm products that reached the tables of urban consumers were our "choice" and "prime" (read "marbled with fat") cuts of meat. When Nebraska-raised corn, soybeans, and alfalfa are funneled into Nebraska beef cattle, we get the famous "Omaha steaks." Those steaks are indeed tender, but I will let you in on a steak secret. Far more delicious steaks come from grass-fed cattle raised in those countries south of our border: Costa Rica, Argentina, and the Dominican Republic. I guess I won't be making any new friends in Nebraska with this chapter. But since the family farms of my youth, with their corn and livestock, have now been taken over by agribusiness conglomerates anyway, I'll be brave and make a suggestion for a healthy change.

It takes 10 pounds of corn to produce 1 pound of beef; perhaps that is why Nebraska farmers feel they need to apply heavy doses of chemical fertilizer, herbicides, and pesticides—so they can produce 8,500 pounds of corn per acre and serve it to all of those hungry cattle eating their way to the slaughterhouse. Why not raise less corn and feed it all to people instead? Think of polenta, cornbread, tortillas, and even corn flakes. Similar cases can be made for soybeans, sorghum, and other grains that are used to fatten livestock but that could just as well be consumed by hungry humans.

I've already mentioned the implications for dietary health that can result from shifting our natural grain production from animal feed to grains for human consumption. But I also have a larger vision in mind: more food to feed those in need around the world; less demand for high-yield, "technified" methods of agriculture; and an incentive to return to "traditional" methods that are kinder to our precious farmlands and those who work our farms. "Sustainable agriculture" is a topic for another book, but you see how related and interdependent are the eating and the production of foods.

Recently, as I mused over this larger world of food, I decided we should take another look at soybeans for our own kitchen. Even my vegetarian partner had dismissed tofu years ago as too bland and too soft to have any place in our diet. Soybeans in our kitchen meant an occasional dash of soy sauce in the stir-fry.

We already knew we *should* be eating soybeans—they're packed with nutrients. It was just a question of *enjoying* them. They are low in flavor. A little investigation, and then experimentation, and we were launched into the most recent healthy change in our kitchen.

We found that tofu is a lot more tasty if you add flavor with a marinade. Soybeans themselves have an intense flavor if they are fermented (that's why soy sauce is tasty, along with miso and tempeh.) I'm still learning variations of miso soup and have extended the experience to include some other parts of Japanese cuisine. Tempeh, lightly roasted after a marinade, quickly became a staple in our house, so I've included it as a last-minute addition to this chapter.

♥♥♥ TEMPEH MARINADE

The tempeh we like best is a combination of fermented soy beans and grains (barley, rice, and millet.) This combination makes for a lower fat content than you would find in a purer soybean product such as tofu. Vary the marinade ingredients any way that suits you. Once roasted, the tempeh is fine by itself, as a snack, or as a side dish. Or use it as an addition to soup or stir-fry.

SERVES 6

    8 ounce package of tempeh, cut into 1-inch strips

FOR THE MARINADE:

1 tablespoon olive oil	1 teaspoon wine vinegar
1 tablespoon fish sauce	1 teaspoon balsamic vinegar
1 to 2 tablespoons lemon juice	2 cloves garlic, chopped
1 teaspoon sesame oil	½-inch slice gingerroot, peeled and
1 teaspoon Worcestershire sauce	chopped
1 teaspoon soy sauce	

Place the tempeh strips in the marinade in the refrigerator, covered, for 8 hours. Bake at 350 degrees F for 10 minutes, then at 300 degrees F for another 10 minutes. The baked tempeh will keep 1 week in the refrigerator.

♥♥♥ HUMMUS

Not long after he emigrated to Vermont from Jerusalem, my friend Mahmoud described this recipe to me one day when we were riding to Ticonderoga together for eye surgery. He says he remembers learning it at his mother's knee in Ramallah, in the West Bank. Any time I've made it, even Mahmoud's wife Salwa swears it's the best hummus she's ever tasted (outside Jordan!), so I think it's a pretty authentic Middle Eastern recipe.

SERVES 10 TO 12 (AS AN HORS D'OEUVRE)

1½ cups dried chick peas (also called garbanzo beans)	3 to 5 cloves garlic
1 cup tahini (sesame seed butter—look for it in natural food stores)	1 to 2 teaspoons salt
	½ cup lemon juice
	½ to 1 cup cooking water (from cooking the chick peas)

Soak the chick peas overnight in water twice the depth of the chick peas. In the morning, drain and replace water, then simmer for 40 to 50 minutes until the peas are nearly tender. Drain, but reserve the cooking water.

Process with a metal blade, the cooked chick peas, tahini, garlic, lemon juice, and enough of the cooking water to achieve a spreading consistency.

Place the hummus on a serving plate and garnish the top with a few chick peas and a drizzle of olive oil.

This freezes very well. You may need to add some water after it is thawed before serving.

Note: If you wish to make *mtabel betanjan* (also known as baba ghanoush), simply substitute baked eggplant for the chick peas in the hummus recipe.

♥♥♥ FELAFEL

This is the other half of the cooking legacy passed on by Mahmoud. The reason both recipes contain chick peas is that this high-protein legume is a staple in the Middle Eastern diet. Hummus is usually eaten for breakfast with pita bread. Felafel is a more festive item—since it requires deep-frying—found at roadside stands or at meals for guests.

SERVES 8 TO 10 (AS A SIDE DISH)

1½	cups dried chick peas	1 to 1½	cups chopped fresh parsley
3	medium onions	½	teaspoon hot pepper
6	cloves garlic	1	teaspoon baking powder
2	teaspoons salt	1	quart peanut oil
2	teaspoons cumin		

Soak chick peas 8 to 12 hours. Drain, but do not cook them. Process the chick peas, along with all the other ingredients except the oil, with a metal blade in the food processor, to a coarse granular consistency. Refrigerate at least a few hours to set. Form into balls 1½ inches in diameter (you may need to sprinkle lightly with water for a good sticking consistency). Deep-fry the balls in peanut oil. A wok works well for the frying. Serve with salsa or tahini sauce.

BEANS

I always thought beans (the dried legumes, that is) were boring. Maybe because I only knew navy bean soup back in Nebraska as a boy. Maybe because I was aware of the gas that beans could produce.

Then I traveled and began to learn about new possibilities in foods. I encountered numerous types of beans and peas—red, pinto, black, cannellini, favas, chick peas, lentils, guandules, cranberry—each different enough for its own place on a menu. Yet all fall into the super-food category in terms of nutrients: they are high in proteins and fiber, rich in B vitamins and minerals, full of complex carbohydrates, and low in fat.

It seems each part of the Third World relies on one or two varieties of legumes for essential nutrients that, when combined with rice or other grains, sustain life when there is no meat and other food is not abundant. *Frijoles* in Mexico and Central America, *habichuelas* in the Dominican Republic, lentils in India, green peas in the English-speaking Caribbean—each has become a habit I could grow to enjoy for daily sustenance. At home, now, we have some form of beans, usually as a side dish, once or twice a day. Any cook with a vegetarian to nourish should take note: the combination of beans and a grain makes a perfect protein as an alternative for meat.

The gas, by the way, is produced by bacteria in our lower intestines that digest certain sugars in the beans not easily digestible by our own gastrointestinal system. The "problem" diminishes when we eat beans in small amounts often rather than only occasionally in a meal based largely on beans. So the old rhyme partly holds—

> Beans, beans
> good for the heart . . .

But as for the results of eating them: the more you eat of them, the less likely you are to have a problem—if you eat them in moderation, of course!

❤❤❤ *HABICHUELAS* (DOMINICAN RED BEANS)

Make this recipe whenever you feel like eating like a Dominican. It's an excellent source of protein, too.

SERVES 9 TO 12 (DEPENDING ON WHETHER YOU USE THIS AS A MAIN DISH OR A SIDE DISH)

- 2 pounds dried pinto or Colorado beans
- 1 cup dried kidney beans
- 1 large onion, chopped
- 3 cloves garlic, chopped
- ¼ cup olive oil or canola oil
- 1 teaspoon crushed cumin seeds
- 1 teaspoon crushed coriander seeds
- 8 to 10 Roma tomatoes, chopped (or a proportional amount of Marinara Sauce; see recipe, page 94)
- ½ teaspoon red pepper flakes
- 1 teaspoon dried oregano
- 2 teaspoons vinegar
- 1 or 2 green or red bell peppers, chopped
- black pepper, to taste
- salt, to taste
- 1 cup cilantro or cilantrico, chopped (cilantrico is the Dominican name for the fine fern-like growth of a cilantro plant just before it blossoms)

The night before you plan to cook this dish, pick any stones or other debris out of the beans, wash the beans, and soak them overnight in enough water to cover. Next morning, discard the soak water, and refill to cover by at least 1 inch. Bring the beans to a boil, and remove any scum that comes to the top. Add the sofrito, described below, and simmer until the beans are almost tender, about 40 minutes (depending on the freshness of the beans).

For the sofrito, sauté the onion and garlic in the oil. Add cumin, coriander, tomatoes, red pepper flakes, oregano, vinegar, bell peppers, and black pepper.

Near the end of the cooking period, add salt and chopped cilantro or cilantrico. Of course, *habichuelas* are commonly served with rice, but also make a side dish for any meat or other casserole meal. They will keep 5 to 7 days in the refrigerator, and in the freezer almost indefinitely.

♥♥♥ RICE

This may seem elementary to include as a recipe, but believe me, I have experienced a lot of gooey, sticky rice messes that were very disappointing. There are as many methods available as there are people cooking rice. This is what we finally found works well for us.

SERVES 6

- 4 cups water
- 1 vegetable bouillon cube
- 2 cups washed rice
- 2 tablespoons olive oil or canola oil

Bring the water with the bouillon cube to a boil. Add the rice. Stir. Bring back to a boil. Continue boiling until the water has disappeared and bubbles form. Add the oil. Stir, cover, and simmer over a low heat for a few minutes. Stir a final time, and cover for another 5 minutes off the heat. Finally, fluff with a fork before serving.

The above method requires about 15 to 20 minutes for white rice. For brown rice, you will need 35 to 40 minutes, and a bit more water.

RICE

Around the world, rice is the Number One food staple. In many Eastern cultures, rice is the core ingredient of three meals a day—other items on the table are considered mere hors d´oeuvres. When we asked our Dominican farm workers for suggestions on the midday meal we provide for them, they asked if we would increase the rice portion from one-half pound each to three-quarters of a pound per person. Never mind the multiple vegetables, or the serving of meat or eggs we were adding to balance the meal. We North Americans are lightweights when it comes to rice consumption.

For all its popularity, rice comes up a bit short in terms of nutrition, thanks to the custom of milling or polishing the husked rice to remove the layers of nutritious bran and germ. The bran, fed to animals, contains all the B vitamins, protein, and several minerals, as well as most of the fiber of the rice grain. The prized white rice ends up with nothing but carbohydrates. So it's essential to combine beans or miso or some other high-nutrient item with the white rice, to replace the nutrients lost by milling. The easier option, of course, is to use brown rice.

But it's hard to get rid of the ingrained notion that "rice is white"—to convince ourselves that brown rice *is* rice. Even though it takes a bit longer to cook, brown rice has a delicious, slightly nutty flavor, along with all the nutrients that are lost in the white polished version.

Short-grained varieties of rice tend to be more sticky when cooked than the long-grained types. So use short-grained rice for sushi, and longer grains when you want the grains separated on your plate. Italian Arborio rice is a stubby, short-grained rice that, due to its extra starch, is the best choice for creamy risotto or for rice pudding.

Wild rice isn't really rice at all, but rather a wild marsh grass native to the Great Lakes region. Its unique nutty taste and texture make it worth the extra cost in certain dishes.

Given the many varieties available and its versatility in so many cuisines, rice deserves a place in your culinary repertoire. Just keep the nutritional factors in mind when you fit rice into your menu, and maybe try the brown version.

♥♥♥ SPINACH LASAGNA OR FETTUCCINI NOODLES

Store-bought pasta just can't compare with noodles made from scratch with either a pasta-making machine or a rolling pin. I'm glad my friends from the office gave us a pasta-rolling machine as a wedding gift. Without it, I may never have been brave enough to try homemade pasta.

YIELDS ENOUGH FOR ONE AND ONE-HALF LARGE (9-BY-12-INCH BAKING DISH) RECIPES OF LASAGNA (SEE RECIPE, PAGE 74)

5	eggs	2	heaping tablespoons
3¾	cups unbleached white flour		chopped, cooked spinach
2	tablespoons olive oil		

Note: You can reduce the number of eggs by substituting 2½ tablespoons of water per egg (I usually use 2 to 3 eggs and substitute water for the remainder.)

Process all of the ingredients in a food processor with a metal blade. Remove onto a floured board and knead until smooth. Cover the prepared dough with a dish towel to prevent it from drying too rapidly. Cut into several pieces, so that each piece is workable either with a pasta-rolling machine or a rolling pin. You'll learn the size of a piece of dough that will conveniently pass through the machine, beginning with setting number one, then progressing through the thinner settings until you reach number six. Then, in the case of fettuccini, pass the sheet of pasta through the cutter. After rolling (and cutting) your pasta, allow it to dry for another 10 minutes.

You may cook fresh noodles immediately, or refrigerate or freeze. Cooking fresh pasta requires only 30 to 40 seconds once the water is boiling. If you plan to make lasagna, drain the cooked noodles and plunge them into cold water containing some canola oil. In the case of fettuccini, drain the noodles and add directly to your sauce.

♥♥ CORNBREAD

Eating fresh cornbread for supper always reminds me that Sara and Berit used to make it as their contribution to our family dinners as a threesome.

SERVES 6

2	cups cornmeal, coarsely ground	1	tablespoon honey
2	teaspoons baking powder	2	tablespoons canola oil
1	teaspoon baking soda	1	egg
1	teaspoon salt	1½	cups buttermilk
1	tablespoon wheat germ or oat bran		

Mix all of the ingredients to form a thick batter. Pour into an oiled 9-by-9-inch-square baking dish. Bake for 25 minutes at 400 degrees F. The cornbread will be easier to remove from the pan if you let it cool a bit before slicing.

♥♥ POLENTA

Polenta became a staple at our house once Julia decided that she was going to join in the cooking effort. We now have it almost every week, especially for Grandpa Eichner, who loves this Italian variety of "cornmeal mush." This dish quickly convinced him that Julia was very much able to cook, too.

SERVES 8

1	cup cornmeal, coarsely ground	½	cup Parmesan cheese, grated
1	tablespoon olive oil	5	ounces Fontina or Gruyère cheese, sliced
½	teaspoon salt		black pepper, to taste
3	cups water		

OPTIONAL:

12	ounces oyster mushrooms, halved and sautéed
3	cloves garlic, thinly sliced

Boil the water, olive oil, and salt. Gradually add the cornmeal, stirring constantly. Lower the heat, and cook until the meal slowly falls off a lifted spoon, about 10 minutes. Spread into a 9-inch-square, oiled baking dish, and chill for at least 20 minutes.

When set, cut the chilled polenta in half. Place one-half on an oiled baking tray. Layer one-half of the sliced cheese on the first layer of polenta along with some black pepper. Stack the second layer of polenta on top and add another layer of sliced cheese and black pepper. Top with Parmesan cheese.

Bake for 20 minutes at 350 degrees F, and then broil for 5 to 6 minutes. You may add mushrooms or garlic before broiling.

BREAD

Bread, for me, is the food of life. My first bread memories are of hearty whole-wheat loaves fresh from the oven of my mother or grandmother on the farm. It smelled and tasted like the wheat we grew. We needed at least a loaf a day to make a nutritious filler for hungry farmers.

In my later years, as a cook and "almost vegetarian," bread has become even more important. Baking it myself is a ritual in our home. Eating bread three times a day makes it the lead item on our table—more important than meat ever was. But to speak of bread in these lofty terms, I'm referring to "good bread." Good bread is a loaf that you can hold firmly in your hand without fear that you'll crush it into a formless paste. Its crust is thick enough to crack as you break or cut it. It has an aroma, not of sugar or water, but a real smell of fermentation and of grain. (I like to be able to detect the presence of the main ingredients in a food.) And when you finally put it in your mouth, good bread has a chewy texture, the flavor of wheat and of the acid and alcohol products of fermentation (not the flavor of yeast).

Good bread doesn't come from any supermarket shelf. Good bread requires an understanding of what makes it good, and the patience and attention that will allow for that goodness to occur. I'm referring to quality wheat flour with sufficient protein to provide the gluten that gives bread its structure. The fermentation process must be natural and slow to provide a pleasantly acidic flavor. And finally, the bread should be baked in a good, hot oven.

The best good bread I've ever tasted was made by a farm woman in the West Bank, the mother of my friend Awni. She mixed a batch every afternoon, using stone-ground wheat from her farm and starter held back from the dough of the previous day. This mixing was followed by the baking of yesterday's dough. Baking was in a *taboon*—a ceramic dome-shaped oven set in the ground, heated by a surrounding bed of coals, fueled by goat dung. White stones on the bottom made the shelf for each single, 2-foot diameter, pancake-shaped loaf. After 5 minutes, Awni's mother picked up the loaf with her callused fingers and flipped it over for another five minutes on the stones. If a hot stone stuck to the loaf she picked it off with her fingers. I've yet to sample bread like that *taboon* loaf just minutes after it was done.

The most time-consuming part of baking bread is the months (or even years) spent learning and perfecting a technique. It's now a routine for me that doesn't crowd my weekend schedule of errands or gardening or entertaining friends. It's essential to my life because of the joy that comes from having such a delicious and nutritious element always at hand.

If you care enough about good bread that you want to learn the technical (and aesthetic) aspects of how and why, have a look at *The Bread Builders* by Daniel Wing and Alan Scott (Chelsea Green, 1999). But beware—this book is so filled with passion and expertise that you may be inspired to drop everything you're doing and devote your life to the baking of fermented hearth bread. I have my own passions, but I plan to read my copy about four more times, then embark on building a masonry oven. I'm still in pursuit of that perfect loaf from the *taboon* oven in Zababdeh, in the West Bank, of twenty-five years ago.

♥♥♥ FOCACCIA

This is a really easy first course that will make people think you can cook just about anything. Think of pizza dough.

SERVES 8

FOR THE DOUGH:

3	cups unbleached white flour		1	teaspoon salt
1⅓	cups water		2	tablespoons baker's yeast
2	tablespoons olive oil			

FOR THE TOPPING:

½	cup plus 1 tablespoon olive oil, divided		2	tablespoons coarse kosher salt
2	tablespoons fresh thyme, chopped		½	teaspoon black pepper
2	tablespoons fresh rosemary, chopped		½	cup sundried tomatoes, chopped
⅓	cup cornmeal		1	medium onion, coarsely chopped

Using a mixer with a dough hook or a food processor with a metal blade, mix the dough ingredients for 7 to 8 minutes (any yeast dough can also be mixed by hand, but will take longer). Remove from the mixer onto a floured surface, and knead by hand until smooth. Place the dough in a large greased bowl, and allow to rise for at least 1 hour.

Combine ½ cup of the olive oil with the chopped herbs in a small non-stick pan. Heat gently. Remove from the heat and let sit, covered, for 15 minutes.

Sauté the onion in the tablespoon of olive oil until transparent, about 5 minutes. Set aside.

Roll the dough to cover a rectangular cookie sheet, or two oven sheets. Sprinkle the pan with cornmeal before placing the dough on the pan. Brush the rolled dough with the oil and herb mixture. Sprinkle with the kosher salt and black pepper. Bake for 12 to 15 minutes at 475 degrees F until golden brown. About 5 minutes before the baking is finished, sprinkle with sundried tomatoes and sautéed onion. Cut and serve while still warm.

♥♥ NAAN

This wonderful oven-baked Indian bread will be the highlight of your Indian dinner menu. I had to go to India to sample and learn about the cuisine to stimulate my desire to make this bread. I hope this recipe will be inspiration enough for you.

SERVES 8

2	cups unbleached white flour	¼	cup milk
1	teaspoon baking powder	¾	cup yeast starter (see
½	teaspoon salt		Sourdough recipe, below) or
¼	teaspoon baking soda		two teaspoons yeast granules
½	teaspoon sugar	about ½ cup yogurt (as needed to
1	egg, lightly beaten		adjust the consistency of the
1	teaspoon oil		dough)

OPTIONAL:

2 tablespoons chopped sautéed onions or garlic
1 to 2 teaspoons herbs (mint, basil, or rosemary)

Place all of the ingredients into a mixer bowl, then mix for 7 to 8 minutes using a dough hook, adding flour or yogurt as necessary to adjust the consistency to form a stiff dough. Onions, garlic, and/or herbs may be mixed in as well. Turn the dough onto a floured board, and knead until smooth. Coat a bowl with oil. Turn the dough into the bowl to coat it. Cover, and let rise for 2 to 3 hours or overnight in the refrigerator.

Heat the oven to 400 degrees F and heat two baking sheets. Divide the dough into eight pieces. Roll each into a triangle. Bake on the hot sheet for 5 to 7 minutes, turning once. At the end of baking, broil for 15 to 20 seconds until brown spots appear.

♥♥♥ SOURDOUGH STARTER

Most of the following sourdough recipes come from a small book that Sara gave me when she was about eight years old called Sunday Breakfast, A Cookbook for Men. *The first recipe under sourdough is sourdough starter. If you can't get a starter from an ancestor (perhaps your father), you can easily make your own. The only other thing to remember is that, whenever you use the starter, save a bit for ongoing stock. You should immediately add some flour and water to the saved portion in order to regain your starter volume.*

1   teaspoon baker's yeast
1   cup unbleached white flour
¾   cup warm water (at about 100 degrees F)

Mix yeast, flour, and water in a medium-sized bowl. Cover the bowl, and leave it in a warm kitchen for at least three days. Stir it a little whenever you remember. When it starts to smell sour, it's sourdough. Put the starter in a pot or jar with a cover. Never fill the jar more than about three-quarters full, or it will overflow when it activates. If you're going to be out of town and not feeding it regularly, stick it in the refrigerator. Otherwise, you can leave it on the shelf and add 2 to 3 tablespoons flour and slightly less water every few days to keep it nourished. If it ever seems particularly lifeless, give it a tablespoon of sugar and another teaspoon of yeast along with the feeding of flour.

♥♥ SOURDOUGH PANCAKES

You will need to prepare for this recipe the evening before you want to make the pancakes.

SERVES 6 TO 8

2½ cups unbleached white flour
2   cups warm water (at about 100 degrees F)
1   cup Sourdough Starter (see recipe, page 66)
1   egg

2½ tablespoons canola oil
¼   cup milk
1   teaspoon salt
1   teaspoon baking soda
3   tablespoons sugar

The night before, combine the flour and water in a large mixing bowl. Add the sourdough starter. Mix with a spoon, just enough to combine the wet and dry ingredients. Cover with a plate, and allow to sit overnight in a warm spot. The next morning, you will find that the mixture has become quite smooth due to the yeast action of the sourdough. If your starter is very sparse, add a little of this mixture back to the starter. Add the egg, oil, milk, salt, baking soda, and sugar to the batter, and mix well. Fry the pancakes on a fairly hot griddle and serve with maple syrup.

♥♥♥ SOURDOUGH FRENCH BREAD

I'll describe the recipe that I use once or twice a week to make bread. This was developed over many years, starting with a variation of Julia Child's French Bread recipe, and finally combining some ideas from a recipe from the New England Culinary Institute, called Hearth Bread.

YIELDS 4 SMALL LOAVES OR 14 ROLLS

6 cups unbleached white flour, divided	1 cup Sourdough Starter (see recipe, page 66)
½ to 1 cup coarse whole-wheat flour	1 teaspoon baker's yeast
3 teaspoons salt, divided	2 tablespoons olive oil
2¾ cups warm water, divided (at about 100 degrees F)	⅓ cup cornmeal

Mix a sponge the night before you plan to bake, by combining 3 cups white flour and the whole-wheat flour with 2 teaspoons salt, 2 cups water, and the sourdough starter. Mix. Cover with a towel and let sit for 10 to 18 hours.

The next morning, prepare the final dough by adding another 3 cups of white flour, ¾ cup warm water, 1 teaspoon salt, and the yeast.

Using a mixer with a dough hook or food processor with a metal blade, mix at low speed for 2 minutes and then at medium speed for 6 minutes. Turn out onto a floured board and knead by hand until the desired consistency is obtained. Add flour as necessary during the mixing. Place the dough into a large bowl that has been coated with olive oil, making sure that the top of the dough is also coated so that it does not become dry. Cover the bowl with a towel, and allow to rise to two or three times the original volume. The speed of the rise can be altered or halted by changing the ambient temperature; the cooler the temperature in the rising area, the slower the rise. The dough can also be placed in the refrigerator to finish rising at a later date.

Punch the dough down briefly. Dump it again onto a floured board. Cut into loaf-sized pieces. You'll learn to form the loaves or rolls that suit you best. I usually bake two small round loaves and about eight rolls. I place the loaves on an oven sheet sprinkled with cornmeal, cover with a towel, and allow to rise a second time, at least 1 hour.

Heat the oven to 425 degrees F. Slash the top of the loaves with a razor or scalpel blade. Place into the preheated oven. Spray every 2 minutes with water until the bread has baked for 10 minutes. Then lower the temperature to 350 degrees F and bake another 15 minutes. Remove the bread from the sheet, and allow to cool on a rack.

♥♥♥ HOMEMADE WHOLE-GRAIN CEREAL

When my daughters were small and I cooked their breakfast each morning, I was certain that they would thrive if they ate cooked oatmeal every day. I found that monotony was not a way to win their hearts at the table, so I tried mixing various grains and other ingredients for a cooked cereal that I hoped would be more appealing. That strategy only worked for a while. Years later, I tasted a mixed-grain cereal meant to be eaten uncooked—the imported Swiss Bircher-Muesli, also called Familia. When I tired of paying seven dollars a pound for it, I decided that I could surely make it myself. Since then, this cereal has been my daily breakfast fare, always topped with yogurt and whatever fresh fruit is in season. The basic ingredients can be found in most any natural food or co-op store.

YIELDS ONE GALLON OR MORE OF DRY CEREAL

6 cups wheat flakes	1 cup dried apricots, chopped
6 cups oat flakes	1 cup walnuts, chopped (or any
1 cup oat bran	other nut you choose)
1 cup sesame seeds	
1 cup dried currants	

Simply mix all the ingredients together—no roasting or toasting is required. Keeps in a closed container almost indefinitely.

CHAPTER SEVEN

ONE-DISH MEALS

T HE RECIPES IN THIS CHAPTER include a wide variety of ingredients and flavors. Their common feature is that they are all nutritionally balanced and appealing enough to stand alone as a meal. Just add salad and/or bread to complete the offering.

Except for pizza and risotto, all of these recipes can be prepared in advance. We often choose from this list when we have guests for the weekend or when we want to prepare to feed ourselves during a week with a heavy schedule.

♥♥♥ SALAD NIÇOISE

This is a wonderful summer main dish. It has so many ingredients that go well together. You can add or delete according to availability and your personal taste. For me, the most important ingredient is small, new potatoes from the garden.

SERVES 4 TO 6

1 to ½ pounds small, new potatoes (any variety)

½ to 1 pound haricots vert (the naturally slender French green bean)

1 large bunch spinach

6 Roma tomatoes, quartered (a few sundried tomatoes will do nicely as a substitute)

juice of 1 lemon (about 2 to 3 tablespoons)

1 tablespoon wine vinegar

1 teaspoon Dijon mustard

¼ cup olive oil

1 scallion, chopped

salt and black pepper, to taste

1 tablespoon capers

OPTIONAL:

1 to 2 grilled chicken breasts, cubed

1 to 2 grilled tuna steaks, cubed

Cook new potatoes unpeeled in boiling water for 4 to 6 minutes, until tender when you pierce them with a fork. Older potatoes will need 10 to 15 minutes of boiling. If you must use older potatoes, it is probably better to peel them after they are cooked, and then slice or cut into small chunks. In any case, it is important not to overcook the potatoes. If you use the green beans, steam them for 3 to 4 minutes, and cut in half. If spinach is used, simply wash, dry, and cut coarsely without cooking.

Add the chopped scallion, capers, salt, and pepper. You may add the tomatoes and chicken or tuna to the above ingredients.

Prepare dressing by mixing the lemon juice, vinegar, mustard, and olive oil. Then add the dressing to the other ingredients and allow to set, marinating for 30 to 60 minutes before serving.

♥♥♥ FETTUCCINI WITH TOMATO AND BASIL SALAD

This is a nice way to combine fresh summer tomatoes with pasta in the form of a main-dish salad for a picnic supper at home or away.

SERVES 8 TO 10

FOR THE DRESSING:

20 large basil leaves	¼ cup balsamic vinegar
3 to 4 cloves garlic	1 teaspoon salt
6 sundried tomatoes (oil-packed variety)	½ teaspoon sugar
	¼ teaspoon red pepper flakes
3 tablespoons olive oil	

FOR THE SALAD:

1 pound Spinach Fettuccini (see recipe, page 62)	6 sundried tomatoes, chopped
	2 pounds plum tomatoes, diced
1 teaspoon olive oil	6 large basil leaves, julienned

To cook homemade pasta, bring a large pot of water to the boil, then add pasta and boil 30 to 40 seconds, until noodles are done but still firm to the bite (*al dente*). Drain and rinse in cold water. Commercial packaged pasta will require 6 to 8 minutes of cooking at a low boil.

Place all of the dressing ingredients in a food processor and purée. Combine the salad ingredients with the dressing, and toss. Serve at room temperature

♥ LASAGNA WITH SPINACH NOODLES

This is the dish we have every Christmas Eve. I also make it for a lot of other special dinners, and always use the homemade noodles from the recipe on page 62.

SERVES 10

15 ounces ricotta cheese	1 quart Marinara Sauce (see recipe, page 94)
4 tablespoons Parmesan cheese, grated	20 to 30 fresh basil leaves (These can be preserved in the summer by carefully packing them in plastic freezer bags and placing in the freezer. They need to be separated very quickly as they are thawing.)
4 tablespoons butter, at room temperature	
salt and black pepper, to taste	
nutmeg, freshly grated, to taste	
8 ounces mozzarella cheese (whole milk or part-skim), grated	
1 pound Spinach Lasagna Noodles (see recipe, page 62)	

Note: You can substitute the commercial variety of lasagna noodles; pre-cook in plenty of boiling water for 6 to 8 minutes, then drain.

Preheat the oven to 375 degrees F.

Prepare the two cheese ingredients in separate dishes. Prepare the ricotta stuffing by mixing the ricotta, Parmesan cheese, butter, salt, black pepper, and nutmeg. Prepare the mozzarella stuffing by mixing the mozzarella cheese with salt and pepper.

Assemble the lasagna in a 9-by-12-inch baking dish, heavily oiled with canola or olive oil. Cover the bottom of the baking dish with a layer of noodles, allowing at least 1 inch of the pasta to hang over the ends of the dish. Cover the pasta with a layer of marinara, and sprinkle with basil leaves. Add another layer of pasta to just cover the tomato sauce, this time with no overhang. Cover the second layer with one-half of the ricotta mixture. Add a layer of pasta, and top it with one-half of the mozzarella mixture. Add another layer of pasta, and cover with marinara and basil leaves. Add another pasta layer, covered with the remaining ricotta mixture, and then another layer of pasta, covered with the remaining mozzarella mixture. Add a final pasta layer, covering the top with tomato sauce. Fold in the remaining edges and cover those with tomato sauce as well. Decorate the top with the remaining basil leaves. Bake the dish in the oven for 25 minutes. Remove, and allow to sit for 15 minutes before cutting and serving.

♥♥ SAFFRON RISOTTO

For me, risotto is an Italian comfort food, even more so than pasta or pizza. It's healthy, economical, allows for a lot of variations, and is relatively easy to fix if you don't mind standing at the stove for 20 or 30 minutes just prior to eating. (The only way to serve risotto is straight from the stovetop.) The idea with risotto, just as with rice pudding, is that you keep heating a rice/liquid mixture, adding the liquid gradually, until each addition is absorbed.

SERVES 6 TO 8

6 to 8	cups vegetable stock
1½ to 2	cups Arborio rice, unwashed
3 to 4	tablespoons olive oil
2	tablespoons shallots, finely chopped
1	cup dry white wine
¼ to ½	teaspoon crushed saffron threads
¼	cup Parmesan cheese, freshly grated
	salt and black pepper, to taste

Prepare the vegetable stock and keep it hot throughout the cooking process.

Sauté the rice in olive oil, in a large flat-bottomed sauté pan. Add the shallots. Cook for 2 to 3 minutes, but do not allow the rice to brown. Stir in the wine, and cook until it has nearly evaporated. Pour in enough broth to just cover the rice, and cook at a gentle simmer while stirring, until the liquid is nearly evaporated.

Continue simmering and stirring, adding approximately 1 cup of stock at a time, never letting the rice become dry. When approximately half the stock has been added, add the saffron threads. After about 20 minutes of cooking, when the rice is slightly creamy, check to see when it is just tender. When you have reached this point, add the Parmesan cheese, salt, and black pepper. Serve immediately.

♥♥ MUSHROOM RISOTTO

We tasted this wonderful, rich-flavored risotto when our friend and Julia's agent Susan Bergholz prepared it for us when we visited her and her husband Bert on Fire Island. We all stood around in the kitchen talking while she stirred for 25 minutes. Remember, when you make risotto for friends, you either leave them in the other room, or they stand around in the kitchen with you while you stir.

SERVES 6 TO 8

2 Portabello mushrooms (or proportional volume of Crimini mushrooms), cut into 1-inch pieces	½ teaspoon white sugar
	2 shallots, chopped
	½ to 2 cups Arborio rice, unwashed
	1 cup dry white wine
2 tablespoons olive oil	6 to 7 cups vegetable stock
3 tablespoons butter, divided	2 tablespoons white truffle oil
salt and black pepper, to taste	⅓ cup Parmesan cheese, grated
½ teaspoon soy sauce	

Quickly cook the mushrooms over high heat in olive oil and 2 tablespoons of the butter, adding salt, pepper, soy sauce, and sugar. Let the water evaporate. Add the additional tablespoon of butter, and the shallots. Cook for another 2 minutes. Add the rice, and cook, stirring, until the rice is just opaque. Add the wine, and cook until nearly evaporated. Then begin sequential additions of broth, and continue cooking until the rice is almost tender but still firm. Remove from heat. Season with salt, pepper, truffle oil, and cheese. Serve immediately.

♥♥ TOMATO AND BASIL RISOTTO

While the saffron and mushroom versions are great in the winter, this risotto is perfect at the end of the summer, made from luscious ripe tomatoes and fresh basil from the garden.

SERVES 6 TO 8

3 to 4 pounds ripe tomatoes (or 2 large cans crushed tomatoes)	6 to 8 basil leaves, whole
4 whole garlic cloves	¼ cup Parmesan cheese, freshly grated
4 tablespoons olive oil	salt and black pepper, to taste
1½ to 2 cups Arborio rice, unwashed	
6 to 8 fresh basil leaves, chopped	

Prepare a broth from the tomatoes as follows: Blanch them in boiling water, peel, mash, and dilute with enough vegetable broth to make very juicy. (If you use canned, crushed tomatoes, no broth will be necessary.)

Sauté the garlic cloves in olive oil in a heavy pan, then remove the garlic and cover the bottom of the pan with 1 inch of tomato liquid.

Lower the heat, add the Arborio rice, and cook in the usual manner for risotto (see Saffron Risotto, page 75), sequentially adding more tomato liquid. Halfway through the process, add chopped basil. At the end, add a few whole basil leaves, along with the Parmesan cheese, salt, and black pepper. Serve immediately.

♥ QUICHE

Julia claims not to have known how to cook until I taught her, but she did bring a few recipes to our marriage! This is one from her earlier life. It's so good that we've never had a desire to change it except that we now add fresh spinach (or dill or parsley when they are in season) to make it a "green quiche."

SERVES 6 TO 8

¾ cup Swiss cheese, shredded	one 10-inch Pie Crust, partially baked (see recipe, page 102)
¾ cup mozzarella cheese, shredded	
	3 eggs, beaten
1 tablespoon green onion, chopped (this may be omitted if desired)	1 cup buttermilk
	½ teaspoon salt
	¼ teaspoon dried oregano

OPTIONAL:

    1 cup spinach
2 to 3 tablespoons parsley, chives, or dill, chopped

Sprinkle both cheeses and the optional onion into the pie shell. Mix together eggs, buttermilk, salt, and oregano, and pour this mixture over the cheese and onion. Sprinkle with chopped greens, if desired. Bake at 325 degrees F for 40 to 45 minutes, until a knife inserted near the center comes out clean. Allow to stand for 10 minutes before cutting.

♥ ONION PIE

This is a perfect one-dish meal that you can make during any season if you have large, sweet onions available. We make it most often in the summer when Walla Walla or Spanish onions are ready in the garden.

SERVES 6 TO 8

6 to 7 medium onions, sliced thin	⅛ teaspoon nutmeg, grated
¼ cup butter	1 tablespoon parsley, chopped
¼ cup dry vermouth	one 10-inch Pie Crust, prebaked
3 eggs	(see recipe, page 102)
yogurt or milk to bring the egg volume to 1½ cups	½ cup Swiss cheese, grated
salt and black pepper, to taste	

Sauté the onions in the butter for about 15 minutes, until tender. Add the vermouth. Boil to evaporate the liquid, and allow to cool. Combine the eggs and yogurt or milk. Add salt, pepper, nutmeg, and chopped parsley to the egg/milk mixture. Spread the onions in the pie crust. Pour in the egg mixture. Cover with the Swiss cheese. Bake at 450 degrees F for 10 minutes, and at 350 degrees F for 15 minutes.

♥ TART SAINT GERMAIN

This is a variation on the onion pie recipe. Using leeks instead of onions brings a bit of elegance to the dish.

SERVES 6 TO 8

6 leeks, sliced thin	1 teaspoon parsley, chopped
½ stick butter	one 10-inch Pie Crust, prebaked
¼ cup dry vermouth	(see recipe, page 102)
3 eggs	½ cup Gruyère cheese, grated
yogurt or milk sufficient to bring the egg volume to 1½ cups	red and green tomato, sliced thin, to decorate the top
salt and black pepper, to taste	
nutmeg, grated to taste	

Sauté the leeks in the butter. Add vermouth, bring to a boil, and cool.
Mix the eggs and yogurt. Add salt, pepper, nutmeg, and parsley.
Spread the leeks into the pie crust, pour the egg mixture on top, add the grated cheese, and finally the sliced tomato. Bake at 450 degrees F for 10 minutes, and at 350 degrees F for 15 minutes.

♥♥ TURKEY AND LEEK SHEPHERD'S PIE

I first tried this in order to make use of Thanksgiving leftovers. It turned out to be a nice kind of comfort food and quite a healthy dish, so I've made it on other occasions as well.

SERVES 10

2 large leeks, thinly sliced	1 cup peas or green beans
2 to 3 carrots, thinly sliced	2 pounds potatoes cooked and mashed
3 cloves garlic, minced	1 cup warm buttermilk or yogurt
2 tablespoons plus 1 teaspoon olive oil, divided	salt and black pepper, to taste
⅓ cup dry, white wine	1 large egg
3 tablespoons white flour	
2 cups chicken or vegetable stock	
2 cups diced, cooked turkey (or chicken)	

Sauté leeks, carrots, and garlic in 2 tablespoons of the olive oil. When tender, add the wine, and cook until most of the liquid has evaporated.

Add the flour, and stir constantly until it starts to brown. Stir in the stock, and simmer for 5 minutes, stirring constantly until the sauce thickens and the carrots are tender. Add the turkey or chicken and the peas or green beans. Remove from heat.

Mash the potatoes with enough buttermilk or yogurt to make a smooth purée. Season with salt and pepper. Beat the egg and 1 teaspoon olive oil into the potatoes.

Place the turkey mix in the bottom of an oiled 9-by-12-inch baking dish, and spread the whipped potatoes on top. Bake at 425 degrees F for 25 to 30 minutes, until the top is golden brown.

❤❤❤ PIZZA DOUGH

This is a simple and quick yeast dough recipe. You can start it 1 or 1½ hours before you plan to construct the pizza.

YIELDS TWO 9-BY-12-INCH PIZZAS

2 tablespoons baker's yeast	2+ cups unbleached white flour
1 cup warm water (at about 100 degrees F)	2 teaspoons salt
	2 teaspoons olive oil
1 teaspoon sugar	

Proof your yeast as follows: Mix the yeast and ½ cup warm water, and add the sugar. Once the mixture is bubbling actively, process with the remaining water, flour, salt, and oil. You may need to add additional flour to achieve proper consistency for the dough. It should be soft and easy to handle, rather than stiff.

Process 6 to 8 minutes with the metal blade (or mix dough by hand), then knead the dough by hand until smooth. Allow to rise 45 to 60 minutes. Roll the dough, and spread onto two baking sheets or tiles. Now you are ready to add toppings of your choice.

❤❤ GRANDMA EICHNER'S PIZZA

I think helping Grandma make her pizza was one of my daughters' favorite child-hood activities (next to eating it). They have told me that hers is still the best pizza they have ever eaten.

YIELDS TWO 9-BY-12-INCH PIZZAS

2 sheets Pizza Dough (see recipe, above)	2 cups mozarella cheese, grated
2 to 3 cups Marinara Sauce (see recipe, page 94)	2 tablespoons fresh basil, chopped
	2 teaspoons dried oregano

OPTIONAL:

1 green or red bell pepper, sliced
1 medium onion, sliced
1 stick pepperoni, sliced

Prepare pizza dough as instructed.

Add a covering of marinara, followed by grated cheese, basil, and oregano. Then add your choice of other toppings.

Bake at 500 degrees F for 10 to 15 minutes.

♥♥ PIZZA WITH PESTO AND SUMMER VEGETABLES

Having a garden leads naturally to variations on a standard pizza. Once you have the dough, you can devise any number of toppings to suit your taste. This one includes a variety of vegetables, and our favorite garden herb, basil.

YIELDS TWO 9-BY-12-INCH PIZZAS

- 2 sheets Pizza Dough (see recipe, page 80)
- 1 cup Pesto, (see recipe, page 96)
- 2 to 3 cups tomato sauce
- 2 cups mozarella cheese, grated
- 1 red bell pepper, diced
- 1 green bell pepper, diced
- 1 small zucchini, diced
- ½ cup black olives, sliced
- ½ cup Parmesan cheese, grated

Prepare pizza dough as instructed.

Spread a mixture of pesto and tomato sauce on the dough. Follow with grated mozzarella and vegetables. Top with grated Parmesan, and bake at 500 degrees F for 10 to 15 minutes.

♥♥ FRENCH ONION PIZZA

This rendition is possible any time of the year. You can always have fresh rosemary if you keep a plant indoors.

YIELDS TWO 9-BY-12-INCH PIZZAS

- 2 sheets Pizza Dough (see recipe, page 80)
- 2 medium onions, sliced
- 2 to 3 tablespoons olive oil
- 3 tablespoons fresh rosemary, chopped
- 1 dozen kalamata olives, chopped
- 1 cup mozzarella cheese, grated
- black pepper, to taste

Prepare pizza dough as instructed.

Sauté onions in olive oil.

Sprinkle the dough with rosemary and olives. Add mozzarella, onion, and black pepper. Bake at 500 degrees F for 10 to 15 minutes.

♥♥ PIZZA WITH EGGPLANT

For those who love eggplant, this pizza is a complete meal.

YIELDS TWO 9-BY-12-INCH PIZZAS

2 sheets Pizza Dough (see recipe, page 80)

1 or 2 eggplants, cut into thick slices

2 to 3 cups Marinara Sauce (see recipe, page 94)

2 cups mozarella cheese, grated

1 or 2 Portabello mushrooms, sliced

oregano or thyme, fresh or dried, to taste

Prepare pizza dough as instructed.

Prebake eggplant for 10 minutes at 375 degrees F, then dice and let cool.

Spread marinara on the dough, add mozarella, and arrange sliced mushrooms and eggplant. Sprinkle with herbs, and bake at 500 degrees F for 10 to 15 minutes.

♥♥ PASTELÓN

This is an elegant and rich main dish that can be prepared ahead. We only see pastelon on the upper-class Dominican tables, because an oven is necessary for the preparation. It is common for the Sunday "family dinner."

SERVES 8 TO 10

FOR THE STUFFING:

½	pounds of chicken breast	1½	cup Marinara Sauce (see recipe, page 94)
2 to 3	medium onions, chopped	1	teaspoon dried oregano
8	cloves garlic, chopped	3	tablespoons Worcestershire sauce
4	chicken bouillon cubes	3	tablespoons vinegar
2	heaped tablespoons fresh cilantro, chopped		salt and pepper to taste
6 to 8	ajises dulces (thin-walled green peppers)	½ to 1	cup water or red wine
10 to 12	Spanish olives, chopped coarsely		
½	cup olive oil, divided		

FOR THE RICE:

3	cups Arborio rice	1	cup plus of cheddar cheese, grated
3	cups water	½	cup Parmesan cheese, grated
1	teaspoon salt		
3	cups whole milk		

Note: Pork can be substituted for the chicken. To make a vegetarian dish, delete the meat entirely and substitute any of the following: habichuelas, guandules, or petit-pois (American-style green peas).

Prepare a marinade for the chicken consisting of ¼-cup olive oil, the vinegar, Worcestershire sauce, oregano, onions, and garlic. Slice the chicken breast to ½-inch thickness and marinate for 8 to 12 hours covered, in the refrigerator.

To cook the chicken, remove from the marinade, brown the garlic and onion in the remaining olive oil, add the chicken slices, cook until just tender, then remove the chicken and cut into pieces ranging from ½ to 1 inch in size. Add the reserved marinade, Marinara sauce, bouillon cubes, ajises, cilantro, salt and pepper to taste. Cook over low heat for 5 minutes until the flavors are well mixed. Add water or red wine for at least a 2 ½- to 3-cup total volume. Add the olives.

Partially cook the rice in salted water, then add the milk and cheese and cook again.

To prepare the final dish, oil a 9-by-12-inch Pyrex baking dish with a bit of olive oil, and layer half of the rice on the bottom. Next, layer all the chicken and add all the sauce save ½ cup.

Add the second half of the rice on top, sprinkle with some grated Parmesan cheese, and drizzle the remaining ½ cup of sauce over the top of the dish. Bake at 375 degrees F for 50 minutes. The top should be browned.

CHAPTER EIGHT

FISH AND MEAT

IF THIS BOOK IS MEANT TO BE a nutritional guide, you may wonder why the fish chapter is so short and the dessert chapter so long. The fact is, living as I do in Vermont, I find it's virtually impossible to have a really diverse fish diet. Coupled with my geographical bias is the sad truth that many of the world's major fisheries—including the Grand Banks off the Atlantic coast of North America—have been in decline for years. This decline, and the depressed state of the fishing industry in general, come as a result of years of over-harvesting a limited resource; ironically, it is our very success in catching fish that now threatens their populations in the sea. The relative scarcity of once-plentiful fish in the market has also driven up the price of fresh fish for consumers.

So, instead of offering many fish recipes, let me take this opportunity to touch on some advice about fish in your diet, both in terms of nutrition and food safety.

The fattier species of fish, for instance salmon, are an important source of omega-3 oil. This unique fatty acid is protective against cardiac arrest due to heart disease. Therefore, since it is low in saturated fats, salmon should be high on your menu list. (Yet another reminder that all fats are not the same.)

Next comes a discussion about food poisoning, since fish can often be a culprit. I must say I've had food poisoning as many times in Vermont as I have in other remote and exotic parts of the world, and it's always been due to the consumption of so-called fresh fish.

Fortunately, the most common kind of food poisoning you'll encounter is brief and benign. If you find a churning and roiling somewhere below your belly button from two to six hours after consuming a meal, you might first assume that it's due to one of several toxin-producing bacteria. The ubiquitous *Staphylococcus* is the most common of these. It will multiply rapidly in any warm, meaty environment, pouring out the chemical toxins for you to consume. In the case of fish, it may or may not have an off-flavor to warn you of the unpleasant consequences. The churning may quickly evolve to intermittent knife-like or twisting pain followed by an episode or two of diarrhea. If your symptoms subside after a couple of hours, you can be fairly confident that you're home free. Be careful not to consume anything other than small amounts of water for the next six hours or so, until your gut has finally rid itself of the toxin and quieted down.

However, if your symptoms persist past six to eight hours, and the diarrhea is severe enough to leave you dehydrated, or if the diarrhea is bloody, you may be a victim of more serious infections such as *Salmonella,* or *Shigella,* or various forms of *E. coli,* and should consult a physician. Meanwhile, once again, don't try to eat or drink anything other than small amounts of water or clear soda.

It is precisely because of fish-borne illness that I debated whether or not to include the recipe for the finest fish I've ever tasted, that is Cousin Ique's Carpaccio of *Dorado*. It would probably be safe to try it if you have a reliable source for fresh fish.

Even in the Dominican Republic, where both saltwater and freshwater fish abound, cooks in the know are very cautious. Even though the actual distance from boat to table may be relatively short, in a tropical climate, many opportunities arise for bacterial infestation. Unpredictable power outages can allow the temperature of fish to rise way above the safe level.

Experienced cooks are also aware of the danger of *ciguatera,* although neither the cook nor the consumer can do much to avoid this type of food poisoning. The disease, endemic in tropical regions, originates from a toxin produced by a sea algae that adheres to dead coral surfaces. When such coral reefs are disturbed, the toxin is spread up the food chain and is concentrated in certain predatory fish such as groupers, jack, snappers, and barracuda. No reliable tests for detecting the toxin have been devised, and the toxin is not deactivated by cooking.

Symptoms of *ciguatera* toxicity begin from one to three hours after ingesting a fish meal. They include not only the typical gastrointestinal problems (nausea, vomiting, diarrhea) but may involve the neurologic system as well, with such symptoms as itching, numbness, and reversal of hot and cold sensation. The disease can be quite severe and long-lasting, and there's no specific treatment. Fortunately, deaths from *ciguatera* are rare.

So caution is advised if you are going to eat tropical reef fish. Do avoid the fish organ meats (for example, liver) and the fish heads. And never eat fish considered dangerous by the local population.

How do you tell if fish is fresh? If the fish counter smells like fish, forget it. The only aroma should be that of the sea itself. Once fish has a fishy smell, it's too late to bother. If in doubt, don't hesitate to get your nose close to the merchandise to check it out (like sticking your nose in a glass of wine to check the bouquet). The appearance is also helpful if the fish is whole. The eyes should be plump and glassy in appearance rather than caved in and hazy. The skin and scales should be glistening and generally moist in appearance.

If you find, as I have in a noncoastal location, that these traits are not consistent, better to forego the fresh variety entirely. Wait until you're traveling on the coast or eating in a big-city restaurant.

♥♥♥ GRILLED TUNA STEAKS

Fish in Vermont presents a real hardship. We're too far from the coast for fresh fish to be a genuine and predictable entity. There is an alternative, however. I occasionally buy 10-pound boxes of vacuum-packed, frozen yellowfin tuna steaks. These are processed on fishing boats in the South Pacific, that is, frozen and vacuum-packed as the fish come out of the water, before the boat ever reaches shore. Compare this to the three- to five-day trip necessary for a fish to reach my local store once it leaves the coastal waters, and you can see why frozen is often far superior to "fresh."

juice of 1 lemon (about 3 tablespoons)	2 tablespoons olive oil
fresh gingerroot, to taste, chopped	¼ cup dry white wine or vermouth
1 garlic clove, crushed	salt and black pepper, to taste
1 teaspoon toasted sesame oil	2 or 3 tuna steaks, frozen and unwrapped

Mix together all the ingredients except the tuna steaks. Place the steaks in the marinade, cover the bowl, and refrigerate for 4 to 5 hours. When ready, grill the steaks quickly over a wood or charcoal fire. Sear both sides to retain the juices. Remove from fire when the center is still pink, about 3 minutes per side.

♥♥♥ CARPACCIO OF *DORADO*

This is Ique's method for fish carpaccio. Ique is our cousin in the Dominican Republic. He started making it when he took up deep sea fishing as a hobby. Carpaccio is any meat sliced very thin, to be eaten raw with oil and spices. Dorado is also called mahi mahi or dolphin (not the mammalian kind). Prepare as much fish as you can catch or buy.

1 part curing salt	1 to 2 tablespoons extra-virgin olive oil
6 parts water	black pepper, to taste
½ part cognac	
dorado filets	

Combine the salt, water, and cognac. Place fresh filets of dorado in the brine. Cover, and refrigerate for 36 to 48 hours. Remove the fish from the brine, and freeze.

When the filets are beginning to thaw, serve thinly sliced, drizzled with extra-virgin olive oil and freshly ground black pepper.

♥♥ ROASTED CHICKEN

This is one of my favorite ways to prepare chicken. Roasting will leave a wonderful fragrance in the house, and the result is the basis for a wholesome and hearty meal of comfort food.

1	whole chicken	2	tablespoons olive oil
2	cloves garlic	½	pound potatoes
2	sprigs rosemary or thyme	½	pound carrots
2	stalks celery		

Preheat the oven to 450 degrees F.

Whether the chicken is fresh, or frozen and thawed, carefully wash the cavity. Check the skin for feathers. Place the garlic cloves, rosemary or thyme, and celery into the cavity for flavor. Brush the skin lightly with olive oil. Place the chicken in the oven on a rack over an oven pan. Immediately lower the oven temperature to 350 degrees F. Baste every 15 minutes or so. Bake about 20 minutes per pound (about an hour and a half for a typical chicken). It's done when the leg flexes easily.

Potatoes can be added about 45 to 60 minutes before the chicken is finished and carrots about 30 minutes before the chicken is finished. Just place them around the chicken on the oven rack. You can test for doneness with a fork.

The chicken should rest about 10 minutes out of the oven before cutting. This will give you time to make gravy from the pan drippings (see recipe, below).

CHICKEN GRAVY

Yields approximately 2 cups

2	tablespoons white flour	small amount of wine or warm water
⅓	cup warm milk or water	
	drippings from roasted chicken (see recipe, above)	salt and black pepper, to taste

Prepare a thickening by stirring the flour into warmed milk or water.

After removing the roasted chicken from its roasting pan (see previous recipe), you will note brown juices and particles in the pan. These provide the rich chicken flavor for the gravy. Place the roasting pan on the burner over medium heat. When the pan is hot, begin slowly adding warm water (or a small amount of wine) to deglaze the pan. Add the thickening mixture very slowly while stirring. Season with salt and black pepper.

♥ POLLO CRIOLLO

This Dominican-style chicken dish is my other great favorite. It's just as wholesome and hearty as American roast chicken, and is sure to leave your stove area nicely grease-splattered.

SERVES 6

1 fresh chicken, cut into pieces

FOR THE MARINADE:

6	tablespoons olive oil		grated nutmeg
2	tablespoons wine vinegar		salt and black pepper, to taste
3	cloves garlic, chopped	⅓	cup white wine

AFTER MARINADE:

1	cup flour	⅓	cup dry vermouth or water
	salt and black pepper, to taste	10 to 12	green olives, chopped
¼	cup plus 1 tablespoon canola or olive oil, divided	8	sundried tomatoes, chopped
		1	tablespoon capers
2	shallots, chopped	1	cup Marinara Sauce (see
2	cloves garlic, chopped		recipe, page 94)

Place a single layer of chicken in a 9-by-12-inch baking dish and cover with the combined marinade ingredients. Marinate for 8 hours or overnight in the refrigerator.

After marinating the chicken, dredge the pieces in flour with salt and black pepper. Brown in a skillet in canola or olive oil. If you are careful to keep the skillet covered, you'll avoid most of the grease splattering.

In a separate pan, sauté the shallots and garlic in olive oil. Deglaze the chicken pan with dry vermouth or water. Add this to the sautéed shallots and garlic.

Add the olives and sundried tomatoes, capers, and marinara sauce, and adjust salt and black pepper to taste. Place the chicken back into this sauce, and simmer until tender, about 30 minutes.

CHAPTER NINE

SAUCES

THIS RECIPE LIST COULD have been longer had I included every sauce that I've ever made and enjoyed. But I've left out white sauces and brown sauces (except for chicken gravy from roast chicken drippings and once-a-year gravy for Thanksgiving), and Hollandaise sauce, all in the interest of healthy change.

Sauces are meant to enhance the flavor of the food they accompany, but in the case of many traditional sauces, that enhancement includes a large dose of saturated fat. To avoid overuse of this ticket to cardiovascular disease, I see two choices. We can choose or devise sauces using monounsaturated oils (olive, canola) and use them sparingly. Or we can use nonfat enhancers such as tomato sauce, lemon juice, nonfat yogurt, and herbs. If we are careful in selection and preparation of the basic food, we may find that a squeeze of lemon is just as tasty as a dollop of Hollandaise.

While we are on the subject of sauce ingredients, let me suggest a radical healthy change for you to consider: *Stop reading labels.* No, I don't mean the name, but rather the ingredient list and "nutrition facts." The way to safely stop reading ingredient labels is to stop buying products with more than three ingredients on the list.

We have an old bottle of prepared salad dressing on our shelf. The label lists fifteen ingredients. Two of the ingredients—corn syrup and anchovy paste—are surprises. One ingredient, called simply "spice," is a mystery. Three of them—propylene glycol alginate, sodium benzoate, and xanthan gum—are downright scary. I've probably spent more time in chemistry classes than most of you, but I'm stumped. How about these three ingredients? One of them sounds suspiciously like radiator antifreeze. I just know that I don't want any of this on my daily salad.

I also don't want to read a lot of other salad dressing labels, because I don't like carrying my reading glasses to the store, and besides, all of the other labels will contain mystery items too. So why don't you start with the two salad dressings in this chapter and avoid the unknown. I checked the label on my bottle of Worcestershire sauce—that one had no mystery chemicals.

If you follow all of the other suggestions in this book for choosing and preparing healthy foods, you won't need the nutrition fact list either. You will learn to balance your choices for nutritional value, replacing more and more of the high-fat or empty calorie items. Keep that goal in mind and you can stop counting calories or fat grams. That will give you more time for reading cookbooks.

HUMBLE BEGINNINGS

by Sara Eichner

I must have been around thirteen or fourteen when my father moved from the country to the only place one could even associate with suburbia in Middlebury, Vermont. He rented a house in, of all places, that very suburban track of 1970s/1980s prefab housing, which will remain nameless here. To a thirteen-year-old, whose perfect family from the country had split up, this place was symbolic of the scary changes occurring to our family.

I tell you this because when cooking for others, you have to keep in mind the baggage your audience brings to the table. As I think about my father's cookbook and his breadth of cooking talents, I can't forget my first encounter with his cooking without my mother around. He'd always been the star when it came to breakfast. But dinner was something I hadn't had to endure from Papa.

The first Wednesday night at Papa's place for dinner illustrates the terror of having to cook for people who depend on you and the horror of having to negotiate the situation as the eater. Dinner in the suburban prefab house was spaghetti and sauce. Now this might be simple if you just employed the magic of Ragú, but if you are Bill Eichner, dinner with the kids requires health and rigor, and nothing out of a jar.

I don't remember the spaghetti; it must have been regular stuff out of a box. However (and I don't know how much of my intolerant, hard-to-please adolescence has to do with this memory, but . . .), the sauce was something to be remembered. There *was* no sauce to speak of; instead, it was some unnamed stew not meant for consumption. Papa had thrown together things like green peppers, zucchini, and mushrooms together to make an unidentifiable lump of something stewlike with a bitter pepper flavor. We were expected to put this mixture on top of the pristine and potentially promising spaghetti and actually eat it. Keep in mind that I am someone who still, at twenty-nine, will not get near zucchini or tomatoes, let alone stewed peppers and zucchini that are meant to resemble marinara sauce. Needless to say, this budding rebellious teenager was further alienated by her father's painful but well-meaning attempt to maintain that family communion. I, however, was an angry teenager, and that dinner lives large in my memory as an adult. It becomes a testament to and a cherished memory of my father learning to cook.

I write this now as my father plans to be in town for a night. He comes at a time when I couldn't be busier, though I look forward to dinner with him as I always have in a way that makes a crazy schedule irrelevant and dinner the ultimate relaxation. Dr. Eichner's cooking skills and advice are invaluable, but what might be missed when looking at a recipe is the value he shared with me and my sister, and the people that have entered my life since that dubious dinner in suburban Middlebury. The meal is only as good as the company and the intent to share that inspires the meal to begin with—whether it is Monday night with your "live-in" or dinner for eight guests who you really want to impress. Basically, the people who are at the receiving end will hold the experience much longer than you might think, even if that person is an insolent thirteen-year-old who will never let you think you're doing anything right.

♥♥♥ MARINARA SAUCE

I make this sauce during the fall, using tomatoes I've frozen during the harvest season. I then preserve it in jars after processing it in a water bath for 10 minutes. It also freezes well. Marinara is a great staple ingredient to make when you find a good source for garden tomatoes, though canned ones work very well.

YIELDS ABOUT 1 QUART OF SAUCE PER 3 POUNDS OF TOMATOES

1 or 2   cloves garlic per pound of fresh tomatoes (according to your taste for garlic), thickly sliced
⅓   cup olive oil
  as many pounds ripe tomatoes as you can find, unpeeled and roughly chopped
  black pepper, to taste
  salt, to taste

Brown garlic in ample olive oil. Add tomatoes. Cook 30 to 40 minutes. Add ground black pepper.

Run the cooked tomatoes and garlic through a food mill to remove most of the skins and seeds. Simmer the juice for 1 to 2 hours uncovered, until desired consistency is achieved. Add salt to taste.

Use for lasagna, pasta sauce, casseroles, soups, or stews.

♥♥♥ SPINACH ARTICHOKE SAUCE FOR PASTA

Julia worked up this recipe for a quick dinner when she went into the food co-op in early May and noted the first local produce of the season—organic spinach. Even though the total time for preparation is 30 to 40 minutes, this sauce is very easy and great-tasting.

YIELDS ENOUGH SAUCE FOR 1 POUND OF PASTA; SHOULD SERVE 6 TO 8

2   cloves garlic, minced
¼   cup olive oil
½   teaspoon dried oregano
1   tablespoon fresh basil, chopped
  salt and black pepper, to taste
1   small can artichoke hearts, cut small

1   small can tomatoes, crushed
1   large bunch spinach, chopped
¼   cup Parmesan cheese, grated
1   cup Marinara Sauce (see recipe, above)

Sauté the garlic in the olive oil in a large saucepan. Add the herbs, salt, and black pepper, along with the water from the can of artichoke hearts. Simmer briefly, then add the can of tomatoes. Simmer for another 30 minutes. Finally, add the artichoke hearts, spinach, Parmesan cheese, and marinara sauce. Simmer for another 5 minutes.

This sauce is good with a medium-sized pasta such as rotini or farfalle.

SEASONINGS

by Julia Alvarez

Style in cooking, as in writing, often does have to do with personal touch. Some chefs put more of this or more of that or an unusual combination of thises and thats that together make for a distinctive burst of flavors in your mouth. In my own native country of the Dominican Republic, a cook is known by her *sazón*—her distinctive seasoning, her signature on the food she cooks up.

"She doesn't know how to cook a whole lot of things, but she sure has good *sazón*," my aunt might say about a new cook she has hired. Good seasoning is like good bones in the face of a would-be model. Surface things can be shifted, hair hennaed or eyebrows plucked. A cook can learn to be more tidy or to make a larger variety of dishes. But if she doesn't have good *sazón*, well, she might as well hang up her apron and go out to McDonald's.

I admit that in my Caribbean desire not to have food taste "American bland," I tended to overdo seasonings when I cooked. (Bill still finds that I overdress salads with too much balsamic vinegar.) I'd wave that shaker of salt or oregano or pepper over my pot of beans as if it were a magic wand. I had a stash of those packets so popular with cooks of my mother's generation, bouquet garni, and a half dozen bottles of chili sauce that I would pour into all my stir-fries. When Bill and I married ten years ago and put our two kitchens together, many of these flavorings went in the trash. What on earth was I planning to do with so much chili sauce? Bill wanted to know.

Being married to someone who introduced me to gardening at the same time as he was teaching me to cook made me into a convert. Nothing is as good as fresh, wholesome food, and seasonings should enhance those natural flavors, not mask them or jazz them up. Too much doctored-up flavor in a dish is like someone wearing too much makeup: you want to shake off that peppery mess with melted cheese and flakes of this and that on top, and just taste that fresh Costoluto Genovese tomato or that leaf of arugula.

Now, if anything, I like to err on the side of simplicity when I season a dish. And as with writing style, I also consider my audience. My mother-in-law dislikes the taste of rosemary and my older sister can't stand nutmeg. I myself am not partial to curry. But having *buen sazón* means a sensitivity to the foods you are cooking as well as to the people who will eat them.

Now, after eleven years of cooking-gardening experience, I tend to agree with my old country's definition of a good cook as someone with good *sazón,* and with my chef husband's belief that a cook should have roots in a garden. Curiously, the root of both words—*seasoning* in English and *sazón* in Spanish—is the Latin word *sationem,* meaning "to sow." To season food is like sowing seeds in the garden: in both cases you want an authentic harvest. After all, you wouldn't want to sow tomatoes and get, well, chili sauce!

♥ PESTO

Another high point in the garden season for me is the time when I can first pick a big basket of basil leaves and make pesto. It's great as a sauce for pasta, and is also a nice addition to some tomato-based soups.

YIELDS APPROXIMATELY 1 PINT

- 3 cups fresh basil leaves, chopped and lightly packed
- 2 cloves garlic
- ½ cup pine nuts (may substitute almonds, walnuts, or cashews)
- ½ teaspoon salt, or to taste
- ¾ cup Parmesan cheese, grated
- ¾ cup olive oil

Process the basil with a metal blade. Add the garlic, nuts, salt, and Parmesan cheese. Process until fine. Stream in the olive oil, and blend to make a smooth paste. In a container, cover with a layer of olive oil. Refrigerate under an airtight cover for several weeks or freeze in small plastic containers for up to 12 months. Frozen pesto will have a better taste and consistency if frozen without the cheese. Add cheese after thawing.

A handy trick is freezing pesto in ice-cube trays, removing the frozen cubes to store in a freezer bag, ready to add to a recipe later in small amounts.

♥♥ RED PEPPER SAUCE

I devised this recipe from scratch after tasting a similar dish in a Boston restaurant. It's great if you like rosemary. We use the sauce on Mostaccioli, but you may use another medium pasta.

YIELDS ENOUGH SAUCE FOR 1 POUND OF PASTA; SERVES 6 TO 8.

- 2 cloves garlic, chopped
- 3 tablespoons olive oil
- 2 red bell peppers, cut into small strips
- 1 to 2 leeks, cut into small strips (include some green)
- 8 to 10 ripe Roma tomatoes, diced
- 1 rosemary leaves, chopped
- black pepper, to taste
- 1 handful of fresh basil leaves, chopped
- salt, to taste
- ½ cup Parmesan cheese, grated

Sauté the garlic in olive oil until tender. Add red bell peppers and leeks. Sauté 3 to 4 minutes. Add tomatoes, rosemary, and black pepper. Cook 2 minutes more but don't let the tomatoes cook down completely. Add the basil and salt. Pour over pasta. Top with freshly grated Parmesan cheese.

♥ MARY MURPHY'S SALAD DRESSING

This is our favorite that we use every day. We double the recipe and keep in a jar on the shelf.

1	clove garlic, minced	2	tablespoons lemon juice
1	teaspoon salt	½	cup extra-virgin olive oil
¼	teaspoon ground black pepper		

Mash the minced garlic with the salt and pepper using a mortar and pestle. Add to a mixing bowl with the lemon juice. Finally, stir in the olive oil.

♥ GRANDMA EICHNER'S VINAIGRETTE

This is a good salad dressing if you want a little stronger flavor, which Julia always does.

2	large cloves garlic, minced	3	tablespoons lemon juice
1	teaspoon salt	1	tablespoon Dijon mustard
½	teaspoon pepper	½	cup extra-virgin olive oil
3	tablespoons balsamic vinegar		dash of Worcestershire sauce

Mash the garlic, salt, and pepper with a mortar and pestle. Turn into a mixing bowl, and mix with vinegar, lemon juice, and mustard. Finally, stir in the olive oil and Worcestershire sauce.

CHAPTER TEN

DESSERTS

I'VE TOLD YOU WHY THE FISH chapter is so short, but I'm having a tough time explaining with a straight face why the dessert chapter is so long. In the end, I can't come up with a single nutritional/medical, or psycho-social justification. I'm afraid I simply have a terrible sweet tooth, and my beloved partner indulges me in this vice.

This "problem" began with our partnership arrangement for cooking: Julia is in charge of desserts and I do a lot of the rest. Since we try to share equally, that means a lot of desserts. My only way out of this conundrum is one more prescription. When you grill tuna steaks, keep all the leftovers to eat during the rest of the week. But when you make a dessert, invite all your friends over and send the leftovers home with them.

You'll note however, that some of these desserts actually have hearts for being "healthy." And they still taste good.

♥ APPLE CRISP

It's wonderful to make an apple pie, but this much quicker recipe still allows you to taste late fall apples, even before you've mastered the art of a pie crust. I would hold out for Northern Spies, Golden Delicious, or Greenings. For the one-heart rating, substitute canola or safflower oil for butter.

SERVES 10

FOR FILLING:

7	cups apples (6 to 8 medium to large apples), peeled and sliced	2	tablespoons lemon juice
		1	tablespoon cinnamon
½	cup brown sugar	½	teaspoon ground cloves
¼	cup currants	½	teaspoon ground allspice
¼	cup nuts, chopped	½	cup yogurt
¼	cup white flour	1	egg, beaten

FOR TOPPING:

1½ cups rolled oats and rolled wheat flakes
¼ cup whole-wheat flour
½ teaspoon salt
1 teaspoon cinnamon
½ cup brown sugar
1 stick (½ cup) butter, melted

Mix the filling ingredients in a rather large container. Do the same for the topping ingredients. Place a thin layer of topping in the bottom of an oiled 9-by-12-inch baking dish. Next spread all of the filling mixture into the dish and cover with the remaining topping. Bake for 30 to 35 minutes at 375 degrees F, until the top is brown and the fruit is bubbling.

♥ RHUBARB CRISP

You may have to be a native northerner to enjoy this. (Sara, you should qualify; rhubarb is one of the few vegetables that grows in Labrador.) To get a heart rating, substitute canola or safflower oil for the butter.

SERVES 10

FOR TOPPING:

1 cup rolled oats	1 cup flour
1 cup wheat flakes	1 stick (½ cup) butter, melted
1 cup brown sugar	

FOR FILLING:

8 cups rhubarb, cut into ½-inch pieces
1 cup white or brown sugar
2 tablespoons flour
juice of 1½ lemons (about 4 tablespoons)

Mix the topping and filling ingredients in separate bowls. Place a small amount of the topping on the bottom of a 9-by-12-inch baking dish. Layer in the rhubarb mixture, then the remainder of the topping. Bake at 375 degrees F for 40 to 45 minutes, until the top is brown and the fruit is bubbling.

Variation: This recipe works well for fresh peaches. In this case, use only ¼ cup sugar for the fruit filling.

PIE CRUST

After trying a variety of recipes, I finally landed on this pie crust tailored for the food processor. It's easy to roll and really never fails. One recipe is enough for a 10-inch crust with a top. I usually double the batch, which is enough for three crusts without tops.

1 stick (½ cup) butter, chilled and cut into tablespoon-sized pieces	½ teaspoon salt
	¼ cup + 1 tablespoon cold water
1 egg yolk	1½ cups unbleached white flour

Place the butter, egg yolk, salt, and cold water into a food processor with a metal blade. Pulse five to six times, then process 5 to 6 seconds. Add the flour, and process until it forms a mass of dough, but not a ball. Immediately turn out onto a floured board. Form into a ball, and then into a disc. Wrap in plastic.

All of the above should be done with minimal touching and manipulation. It's important to keep all the ingredients cold. Excessive pushing or kneading will result in a tough crust. Refrigerate for at least 2 hours, or overnight, or freeze.

To roll the chilled dough, dust both sides, your smooth work surface, and the rolling pin with flour. Then use the rolling pin to press the thick disc into a slightly thinner disc before you begin rolling. Check often that the crust does not stick to the work surface or the pin (use additional flour). Gently begin rolling with short strokes from the center outward to gradually thin the dough into a round crust. Occasionally roll along the round edge to keep it smooth. Check the result against the pie plate so you stop before it's too large (and too thin). Don't panic if a tear or buttonhole forms, just patch and press, keeping in the mind the admonition: minimal touching and manipulation. Partially roll the crust around the pin in order to transfer to the pie plate. Center the crust in the plate, trim off large excesses, and smooth the edge. Crimp the edges with your fingers or a fork.

Refrigerate the crust for 30 minutes. Prick the bottom and sides with a fork.

If your recipe calls for an unbaked crust, it's now ready to fill. If you need a prebaked crust, first line the crust with aluminum foil, and fill with beans or rice to keep the bottom flat. Bake at 400 degrees F for 12 minutes, and then empty out the beans and bake for 6 minutes more.

Note: To make pie pastry cutouts, roll a piece of crust, then use a small glass or cookie cutter to press out shapes to use on top of a pie.

MOM'S PIE CRUSTS

by Ruth Eichner

My mother's teaching me to make pie crust on the farm in Nebraska in the early 1930s was not easy. No refrigeration for chilling the greasy home-rendered lard, not even a measuring cup. Just a pile of this and a pile of that—about "so big." What a lesson for a thirteen-year-old! Later, as I saved my pennies and bought a measuring cup, and Crisco and Spry came on the market with a real recipe on the can, my pie crusts improved. So now, in my eighties, I'm not happy with any other ingredients, even though I know that Crisco is not the healthiest type of fat. I want the flaky crust that comes with cutting in the shortening with my ancient wood-handled two-tined meat fork. After all, the small portion of Crisco in one piece of pie won't harm my family and friends too much.

My second son Steve has what he says is the best pie crust recipe, because it is easiest, fool-proof even for a novice, and the best healthwise. My two daughters, Faith and Laura, are happy enough using my Crisco recipe because that is what I taught them when they were girls about the same age as I had been when my mother taught me. My other child, David, is not a cook, but he's happy to eat any pie crust the family produces.

Steve's pie crust:
Whisk together:

2 cups flour

1½ teaspoons salt

Combine in cup:

½ cup canola oil

5 tablespoons milk

Add all at once. Mix, form into a ball, then divide in two. Put between two 12-inch squares of waxed paper, and roll out. As dough forms a circle reaching the edges, it is the correct thickness and size. Peel off the top paper and then flip the crust into a 9-inch pie pan.

My pie crust:

1¼ cup Crisco vegetable shortening

3 cups flour

1½ teaspoons salt

⅓ cup or more of water

Cut in shortening with flour until the consistency of coarse cornmeal. Using both hands, add water gradually until it forms a solid mass. Divide into three equal parts, and pat each into a small, flat round. Wrap each in plastic wrap or waxed paper. Chill. I like to keep several pieces in the freezer so I can have them ready when I need a pie.

PUMPKIN PIE

This recipe is from Grandma Eichner. She can never allow Thanksgiving to pass without one or two of these pies. As noted below, I prefer some additional spices to increase the flavor a bit.

MAKES 1 PIE

one 10-inch pie shell, unbaked
    (see recipe, page 100)
1 tablespoon butter, melted
2 plus cups pumpkin, cooked
¾ cup dark brown sugar
½ teaspoon salt
1 to 2 teaspoons cinnamon
1 to 2 teaspoons ground ginger
¼ to ½ teaspoon nutmeg

¼ teaspoon cloves (optional)
¼ teaspoon allspice (optional)
2 ounces dark molasses
    (optional)
1 cup milk, scalded
1 small can (5 ounces)
    evaporated milk
3 eggs, beaten

Brush the pie shell with melted butter then refrigerate.

Cook the pumpkin, brown sugar, salt, spices, and molasses in a saucepan over moderate heat until thick, about 5 to 7 minutes. Stir in the two kinds of milk and the eggs, and cook over low heat for another 5 minutes. Pour into the pie shell, and bake for 15 minutes at 425 degrees F, and then at 350 degrees F for 45 minutes.

PUMPKINS

I'm glad that I have growing space outside my garden proper. I've tilled five long strips in the old pasture that runs below our house and garden. I rotate planting the strips, alternating legumes (alfalfa and red clover) to replenish the soil with nitrogen and organic material, with crops that need a lot of space such as sweet corn, potatoes, and pumpkins. Pumpkins like to roam, their vines extending up to 20 feet in any direction. Don't ever plant them next to your tomatoes.

In years past when my girls were small, I wanted big pumpkins for carving. Known as cow pumpkins, they have names like Big Moon and Dill's Atlantic Giant. Once my family outgrew jack-o'lanterns (well, almost) I started selecting my pumpkin varieties for flavor rather than size. The best pie varieties are only 8 inches in diameter, with coy names like Small Sugar, or elegant names that sound aristocratic, like the French heirloom Rouge Vif d'Etampes. Their sweet flavor is also great for soup and cake.

It's time to add some drama to the garden this year, so I'm planting pumpkins. Maybe we'll make more jack-o'lanterns when the harvest comes in, but they'll be small. I'm leaving the cow pumpkins for the cows!

RASPBERRY GLAZE PIE

This is an impressive crowd pleaser and very easy to make. The only catch is that you need fresh raspberries.

MAKES 1 PIE

¾ cup white sugar
1½ tablespoons cornstarch
¾ cup water
½ package (3 tablespoons) raspberry Jell-O
1 tablespoon butter

juice of ½ lemon (about 1 tablespoon)
1 quart fresh raspberries (or strawberries)
1 baked pie shell (see recipe, page 102)

Thoroughly mix the sugar and cornstarch, then mix in the water. Cook, stirring constantly, to boiling, then continue to cook and stir until the mixture is thick and fairly transparent. Remove from the heat. Add the Jell-O, butter, and lemon juice while the mixture is still hot, to dissolve the Jell-O and melt the butter.

Fill the pie crust with the raspberries. When the glaze mixture is nearly cool, pour it over the fruit. Serve with whipped cream.

RHUBARB CUSTARD PIE

I don't know whether the fact that this is Grandma Eichner's recipe will ever convince you to try rhubarb, but I sure recommend it.

4+ cups rhubarb, cut into ½-inch pieces
1 unbaked pie shell (see recipe, page 102)
1½ cups white sugar
4 tablespoons flour
½ teaspoon nutmeg

1 tablespoon butter, softened
2 to 3 eggs, beaten
pastry cutouts (see recipe, page 102)
milk
sugar

Spread the rhubarb into the pie shell. Mix the sugar, flour, and nutmeg. Add the butter and eggs. Pour the mixture over the rhubarb. Place pie pastry cutouts on top of the pie. Brush with milk. Sprinkle with sugar. Bake at 450 degrees F for 10 minutes, and then at 350 degrees F for 30 minutes, until the center is bubbling.

CHEESECAKE

I would usually prefer a flan or bread pudding or fruit dessert, but I suppose there's always some occasion when a cheesecake is just the right thing.

SERVES 8 OR 10

FOR CRUST:

- 1¾ cups graham crackers, crushed
- ¼ cup walnuts, ground
- ¼ teaspoon cinnamon
- 2 sticks (1 cup) butter

FOR FILLING:

- 16 ounces cream cheese
- 1 cup sugar
- 3 eggs
- ¼ teaspoon salt
- 2 teaspoons vanilla
- ½ teaspoon almond extract
- 3 cups sour cream

Blend the crust ingredients using a metal blade in a food processor. Reserve 1 tablespoon of the mixture, and press the remainder over the bottom and sides of an 8½-inch spring pan.

Blend together all of the filling ingredients, reserving the sour cream for the end. Pour the filling into the crust. Sprinkle with the tablespoon of reserved crust mix. Bake at 375 degrees F for 50 minutes. Remove from the oven, and chill for 5 to 6 hours before removing the sides of the spring form.

APPLE CAKE

I first made this for Julia's father's birthday when he made a visit to Vermont shortly after our marriage. Now Julia, the dessert chef, makes it for me.

SERVES 10

FOR FILLING:

- 3 pounds apples, peeled and sliced
- 1/4 cup sugar
- ½ cup water
- ½ lemon, sliced
- ½ cup currants
- 3 tablespoons dark rum

FOR PASTRY:

- 2 cups unbleached white flour
- 1 cup sugar
- ½ teaspoon salt
- 1½ teaspoons baking powder
- ½ teaspoon cinnamon
- 1 stick (½ cup) butter, chilled
- 1 egg
- 3 drops almond extract

FOR TOPPING:

- 1 tablespoon dark brown sugar
- pinch cinnamon

For the filling, simmer the apples with the sugar, water, lemon slices, and currants (plumped in the rum). Cook for only a short time, until the apples are just tender.

To prepare the pastry, mix the dry ingredients with the butter until crumbly. Then add the egg and almond extract to moisten. Reserve one cup of the pastry mixture and press the remainder on the bottom and sides of an 8½- or 9-inch spring pan.

Drain the apple mixture, discarding the lemon slices. Fill the crust with the apple mixture. Spread the extra cup of pastry mixture on top. Sprinkle with the combined topping mixture. Bake at 350 degrees F for 1 hour.

by Julia Alvarez

I didn't grow up with apples in the Dominican Republic. Instead we ate the native fruits: mangoes, pineapples, oranges, sweet lemons, *nisperos,* and, my favorite of all, guavas. Apples were the red fruit shown in the hands of a sheepish Adam and Eve in my catechism book as they were marched out of Paradise.

My only encounters with apples had not left a good taste in my mouth. Every December, mealy, dented apples would appear at Wimpy's, the one fancy *supermercado* in the capital, and my mother would buy a few. *Manzanas,* along with nuts and dates, were a Christmas treat. And so my first experience of apples was as a festive fruit that was, nevertheless, not very good. Why would Adam and Eve give up happiness for such a mediocre fruit? I wondered.

How wonderful now to live in Vermont where apples come in all kinds of shapes and delicious varieties. My first experience with this cornucopia of apple possibilities came through a small orchard in Cornwall, Vermont, owned by a colleague of my husband, Dr. Ted Collier. Every autumn for two weekends in a row in mid-September, Ted used to open up his orchard to his doctor friends and their families.

For me, those Collier apple-picking weekends always signified fall: We headed out to Cornwall on a crisp, bright afternoon with two boxes in the trunk and a bag of Dominican coffee for Ted and Joan. I would spot Ted in his baseball cap, making cider in the barn or propping up a ladder against the side of a tree. Somehow he always had a minute to say hello and give us the latest apple-harvest bulletin. It was Ted who introduced me to what has become my favorite apple, actually my current favorite fruit: the Russet apple.

We were invited to pick only Macs and Cortlands, but Ted allowed us to collect drops from any other trees. One time I found a small, brownish apple under a tree, and when I bit into it, my mouth filled with a tart, sweet flavor that took me all the way back to my childhood in the Dominican Republic. It was the taste of a certain kind of firm, flavorful guava that I could not get in Vermont. I asked Ted about the apple, and it turned out to be a Russet. He had several trees that he had planted in the orchard, for they were his wife Joan's favorite apple.

"I hope you don't mind if I pick the drops?" I asked.

"They're all yours," he said, "every one."

And so, every year, when we arrived at the orchard, I headed toward those trees, hoping, just hoping, that the night before a strong wind had increased those apple drops.

"Get any Russets?" Ted would ask me as I climbed the small rise toward where our car was parked. Every year, he'd give me a taste of a new find, a Pound Sweet or a Gravenstein or a Northern Spy he thought I might like as much as a Russet. I always savored and complimented, but in the end, I'd shake my head and say, "I still agree with Joan. Russets are the best."

Now, I understand Adam and Eve's predicament a lot better. Surely, those tempting apples must have been Russets?

APPLE-WALNUT CAKE

This impressive recipe from Grandma Eichner is something like a fancy carrot cake made with apples. The best varieties are the hard flavorful ones—Greenings, Golden Delicious, and Northern Spies. Black walnuts are not easily found in the markets. You can find them in some specialty food stores and mail-order catalogs. They have a unique and intense flavor compared to the common English walnut. My mother grew up with them in Nebraska and wouldn't use any substitute. That means my father had to find a black walnut tree, collect the nuts in their black hulls, dry them, hull them, dry them again, crack them with a hammer, and then go at the tedious task of picking the nuts free of the woody shell. Another reason this dessert comes under the category of impressive.

SERVES 10

FOR CAKE:

3 large eggs, beaten	2 teaspoons cinnamon
2 cups sugar	½ teaspoon nutmeg
½ cup plus 1 teaspoon canola oil	¼ teaspoon salt
2 teaspoons vanilla extract	4 cups apples, diced and peeled
2 cups unbleached white flour	1 cup black walnuts, coarsely
2 teaspoons baking soda	chopped

FOR FROSTING:

6 ounces cream cheese, softened at room temperature
½ stick (¼ cup) butter, softened at room temperature
1½ cups powdered sugar
½ teaspoon vanilla extract

Note: "creaming butter with sugar" means mixing in a way so that the butter actually coats the sugar. This requires that the butter be sufficiently softened, but not melted. You can hurry this process by cutting it into tablespoon-sized pieces. If the ingredients are at the correct temperature, the mixture will be thick and smooth.

With a mixer, combine the eggs, sugar, ½ cup of the canola oil, and vanilla extract. Blend in the flour, baking soda, cinnamon, nutmeg, and salt. Fold in the apples and walnuts. Bake in a 9-by-12-inch baking dish, greased with 1 teaspoon canola oil, at 325 degrees F for 50 to 60 minutes. Let cool completely before frosting.

For the frosting, cream together the cream cheese, butter, and powdered sugar. Add the vanilla extract.

It will be easier to frost the cake if both the frosting and the cake are at room temperature. Place a large blob of frosting on top of the cake, and level the icing over the surface with a spatula or large knife until the cake is entirely covered. Refrigerate the cake for about 10 minutes to let the icing set.

CARROT CAKE

This is Grandma Eichner's recipe. To make it authentic, you'll have to find black walnuts, the ultimate product of the Midwest. English walnuts will work, but do not have as distinct a flavor.

SERVES 10 TO 12

FOR CAKE:

2¼ cups unbleached white flour
2 cups white sugar
2 teaspoons baking soda
1 teaspoon ground cinnamon
½ teaspoon salt
4 eggs

1⅓ cups canola oil
1 cup black walnuts, coarsely chopped
2 cups carrots, grated (about 1 pound before peeling)

FOR FROSTING:

½ stick (¼ cup) butter
6 ounces cream cheese
1½ to 2 cups powdered sugar
1 teaspoon vanilla extract

In a large bowl, combine the flour, sugar, baking soda, cinnamon, and salt with a mixer. Combine the eggs and canola oil in a separate bowl. Then mix the wet and dry ingredients together well with the mixer. Add the walnuts and grated carrots. Bake in a 9-by-12-inch greased pan at 350 degrees F for 50 minutes, or until a toothpick inserted into the center comes out clean.

To make the frosting, cream together the butter, cream cheese, and powdered sugar (see note on creaming, page 109). Add the vanilla extract. Frost the cake when it has cooled.

Note: Instead of the single flat cake, this recipe can be made in two layers using 8-inch round cake pans. In this case, add a layer of frosting in between the two layers of cake.

Additional Note: Delete the frosting (I can't), and this cake is easily worth one heart.

♥ PUMPKIN-PECAN SPICE CAKE

This is a very straightforward recipe despite the many ingredients. The cake is dense, with a wonderful spicy flavor. It stays fresh for many days.

SERVES 12

2 sticks (1 cup) butter	1 teaspoon salt
1¼ cup white sugar	2 teaspoons ground cinnamon
½ cup dark brown sugar	½ teaspoon ground ginger
4 large eggs	½ teaspoon ground allspice
1⅔ cups pumpkin, cooked	½ teaspoon ground nutmeg
½ cup yogurt	½ teaspoon ground cloves
¼ cup unsulfured molasses	1½ cups chopped pecans
2 tablespoons dark rum	½ cup crystallized ginger, minced
3½ cups flour	2 tablespoons powdered sugar
2 teaspoons baking soda	
2 teaspoons baking powder	

Cream together the butter, white sugar, and brown sugar in a large mixing bowl (see note, page 109). Add the eggs, pumpkin, yogurt, molasses, and rum. Mix in the flour and remaining dry ingredients. Bake in a Bundt pan at 350 degrees F for 1 hour. Sprinkle with powdered sugar. Serve with Ginger Whipped Cream (see recipe, page 121).

To earn a heart for this recipe, you'll need to omit the whipped cream, and substitute canola oil for some of the butter.

♥ CRANBERRY GINGERBREAD

Here we dress up an old traditional recipe by adding the tangy flavor of cranberries, a very traditional New England product. Be sure to drop a few bags of cranberries into the freezer when they're available at Thanksgiving. They work great for any recipe straight from the freezer.

SERVES 10 TO 12

3 cups unbleached white flour	2 eggs
1½ teaspoons baking powder	1 cup +2 tablespoons molasses
1½ teaspoons ground cinnamon	1 cup +2 tablespoons buttermilk
1½ teaspoons ground ginger	2½ cups cranberries, coarsely
¾ teaspoon ground allspice	chopped
¼ teaspoon ground cloves	⅓ cup crystallized ginger
¾ teaspoon baking soda	1 to 2 tablespoons fresh
¾ teaspoon salt	gingerroot, chopped
1½ sticks (¾ cup) butter	(be brave)
¾ cup dark brown sugar, packed	

Sift all of the dry ingredients into a bowl.

With a mixer, cream the butter and brown sugar in a large bowl until light and fluffy (see note, page 109). Beat in the eggs one at a time. Add the molasses. Then mix in the dry ingredients alternately with the buttermilk, beginning and ending with the dry ingredients. Finally, fold in the cranberries and two kinds of ginger. Pour into a greased and floured 9-by-12-inch baking dish. Bake at 350 degrees F until springy to the touch (about 50 minutes). Cool in the pan on a rack. Serve with Brown Sugar Whipped Cream (see recipe, page 120).

TITA'S FLORENTINE POLENTA CAKE

One of Tita's supposedly simple, but very elegant desserts. She claims this is her favorite cake. At any rate, it has a unique and superb flavor/texture combination.

SERVES 10

2 teaspoons anise seed, crushed	peel of one lemon, grated
2½ cups confectioner's sugar	2 eggs plus 2 yolks
1 stick (½ cup) unsalted butter	1½ cups cake flour
1 teaspoon vanilla	1½ cups yellow cornmeal

One day ahead, mix the crushed anise seed with confectioner's sugar and allow to stand. The following day, cream the butter with the anise sugar (see note, page 107). Then add vanilla and lemon peel. Beat in two eggs one at a time, then two yolks one at a time.

In a separate bowl, sift together the cake flour and cornmeal. Add the flour mixture to the egg/butter/sugar combination, ½ cup at a time. Mix well; this batter is very thick. Pour into a greased 8- to 9-inch round cake pan.

Bake at 325 degrees F for 35 to 40 minutes, until a toothpick inserted into the center comes out *almost* clean. It is important not to overbake.

CHOCOLATE CAKE

When Julia and I met, I had a chocolate cake recipe that contained mayonnaise to make it moist. When we married, and Julia moved in, all mayonnaise moved out of the house, so this is her non-mayo alternative.

SERVES 10

FOR CAKE:

2 sticks (1 cup) unsalted butter	½ cup buttermilk (a small amount of milk added to yogurt will do nicely)
1 cup hot water	
¼ cup cocoa	
2 cups unbleached white flour	2 eggs
2 cups white sugar	1 teaspoon vanilla extract
1 teaspoon baking soda	

FOR FROSTING:

4 ounces semi-sweet chocolate
½ stick (¼ cup) butter
3 tablespoons yogurt
⅔ cup (or more) powdered sugar
1 teaspoon vanilla extract

To make the cake, melt the butter, and add the hot water and cocoa. Bring this mixture to a boil. Set aside to cool.

Combine the flour, white sugar, and baking soda. Then add the heated butter-cocoa liquid, and stir. Next, add the buttermilk, eggs, and vanilla extract. Stir well. Pour into a 9-by-12-inch baking pan or two round cake pans. In either case, the pans should be oiled, and if using round cake pans, lightly floured. Bake at 350 degrees F for 20 minutes.

For the frosting, melt the semi-sweet chocolate in the butter. Remove from the heat, and beat in the yogurt, vanilla, and powdered sugar, until the desired consistency is achieved. Beat until smooth, and pour on while the cake is still a bit warm.

DATE CHOCOLATE-CHIP CAKE

This recipe, like many, comes from Grandma Eichner. It's one of those quick and easy recipes that never fails to please or come out just right.

SERVES 10

1½ cups boiling water
1 cup chopped dates
1¾ teaspoons baking soda, divided
1 stick (½ cup) butter
1 cup white sugar
2 eggs

1¼ cups + 3 tablespoons unbleached white flour
¼ teaspoon salt
½ to 1 cup chocolate chips
½ cup nuts, chopped
½ cup brown sugar (preferably Dominican)

Pour the boiling water over the dates with one teaspoon of the baking soda.

Cream the butter and white sugar in a large mixing bowl (see note, page 109). Add eggs and beat well. Add the dates to the egg mixture. Blend in the flour, salt, and an additional ¾ teaspoon baking soda. Pour the mixture into a greased 9-by-12-inch baking dish. Sprinkle the chocolate chips, chopped nuts, and brown sugar on top of the batter. Bake at 350 degrees F for 30 to 40 minutes. No frosting is needed, as the latter additions make a nice topping.

CHOCOLATE-CHIP OATMEAL COOKIES

My daughter Berit used to make hundreds of chocolate-chip cookies for me. It was such a popular recipe for us that I finally insisted we add some oatmeal to dilute the sugar and fat a bit.

YIELDS 2 TO 3 DOZEN COOKIES, DEPENDING ON SIZE

2 sticks (1 cup) butter
1½ cups brown sugar, firmly packed
2 eggs
1 teaspoon vanilla extract
1 teaspoon baking soda, dissolved in 2 tablespoons warm water

1⅓ cups unbleached white flour
3 cups rolled oats
1 cup nuts, chopped
1½ cups chocolate chips

Cream the butter and brown sugar together (see note, page 109). Beat in the eggs one at a time. Add the vanilla and baking soda dissolved in water.

Finally, stir in the flour, rolled oats, nuts, and chocolate chips. Spoon the dough onto a greased cookie sheet, arranging the cookies 2 inches apart. Bake for 8 to 10 minutes at 375 degrees F.

BROWNIES

Everybody needs a favorite brownie recipe for a comfort dessert. This is what we've come up with after lots of adjustments. It also freezes well.

YIELDS FIFTEEN TO EIGHTEEN 2-BY-3-INCH BROWNIES

1 stick (½ cup) butter	2 cups white sugar
4 ounces unsweetened chocolate	1 teaspoon vanilla extract
3 eggs, at room temperature	1 cup unbleached white flour
¼ teaspoon salt	1 cup nuts, broken

Melt the chocolate in the butter and let cool.

Beat the eggs, and add salt, sugar, and vanilla. Mix the chocolate and egg mixtures, and fold in the flour and nuts. Spread into a 9-by-12-inch baking dish. Bake at 350 degrees F for 22 to 25 minutes. Cut into pieces as soon as the brownies begin to cool. Put into the refrigerator to keep the brownies chewy.

BREAD PUDDING

This recipe was a collaboration among Tia Rosa, Mami, and her wonderful cook Ana in Santiago. After some trial and error and alterations, we came up with this consistent crowd-pleaser. It's also quick and easy. By far the best bread to use is day-old sandwich bread, from a good bakery (such as Baba à Louis in Rutland, Vermont). You might have to search for pasta de guava *(a very dense preserve commonly found in the markets in the Dominican Republic)—perhaps in ethnic food stores. Otherwise, substitute a fruit preserve from the supermarket.*

SERVES 10 TO 12

6 cups whole milk	peel of 1 lemon, grated
1¾ cups white sugar	6 ounces prunes, chopped
½ teaspoon salt	4 eggs, beaten
1 stick (½ cup) butter	1 loaf stale white bread, cubed
1 teaspoon ground cinnamon	with crusts removed
1 teaspoon vanilla extract	8 ounces guava paste
¼ cup dark rum	⅓ cup brown sugar

Heat together the milk, white sugar, salt, butter, cinnamon, vanilla, rum, lemon peel, and prunes. Finally, add the eggs. Pour this mixture over the bread in a large bowl and soak for 15 minutes. Then place the entire mixture in a 9-by-12-inch oiled baking dish. Cut the guava paste into small strips, and press into the top of the mixture. Sprinkle Dominican brown sugar over the top, and bake at 375 degrees F for 50 to 60 minutes.

Note: Substitute one half cup of canola oil for the stick of butter to allow at least one heart for this dessert.

♥ RICE PUDDING

Julia learned this recipe from Mami when she was visiting at our house. The proper name is Arroz con Leche.

SERVES 6

4 cups whole milk	1 cinnamon stick
1 cup Arborio rice	¼ cup white sugar
2 cups water	1 teaspoon vanilla extract
⅛ teaspoon salt	1 teaspoon ground cinnamon

Heat the milk in a large saucepan, and maintain its heat while preparing the rice pudding.

In a second saucepan, mix together the rice, water, salt, and cinnamon stick. Bring to a boil, then lower heat to a simmer for the rest of the process.

Slowly begin to add the warm milk, approximately ½ cup at a time, stirring constantly. Let most of the milk absorb before adding the next portion. With the last addition of milk, add the sugar and vanilla. Raise the heat briefly, and continue to stir. Remove from heat while the pudding is still very soupy. This requires from 20 to 22 minutes after the water has begun to boil. Sprinkle with ground cinnamon before serving.

ARROZ CON LECHE

by Julia Alvarez

I don't know where I got the idea that this is the dessert by which a girl proves she is ready for marriage.

I think Mami put this story into my head. Whenever she wanted to encourage my domestic arts, she'd sing me a little song called *Arroz con Leche* [Rice Pudding]:

> Arroz con leche se quiere casar
> con una muchacha de la capital
> que sepa coser, que sepa bordar
> que ponga la aguja en su mismo lugar.

> Rice and milk wants to marry
> a girl from the capital
> who knows how to sew and how to embroider,
> who puts away her needle where it belongs.

Mami warned that I better learn to cook (and sew and embroider and iron) or I'd never get a husband. The telling art would be making a good rice pudding.

But I was interested in other arts, and so I made myself clumsy in the house. I didn't want be trapped in the one vocation Mami said girls could have. The result is that I never learned how to cook as a girl. Instead, it wasn't until I married in my late thirties to a man who was a good cook that I begin to be interested in Dominican cooking.

He wanted to learn some recipes from me, and I knew none. On a trip to the Dominican Republic, Mami cooked Bill some *arroz con leche,* and he couldn't believe how good it was. And healthy. This six-serving recipe for rice pudding contains—in all— one-quarter cup of sugar. The trick is in the stirring until the milk thickens and becomes pudding.

There's not much to *arroz con leche* but patience. You do have to stand by the stove and stir and stir and stir—a good twenty minutes to half an hour. If you are willing to do this for your honey, maybe it is time to move in with him.

♥ TAPIOCA PUDDING

I think this old-fashioned dessert fits into that small category that we can call healthy. Tapioca pearls are made from the juice of yucca (a common root crop staple in the Dominican Republic), also known as manioc in the South Pacific.

SERVES 8

1 cup tapioca (I like the large pearls)	½ teaspoon salt
	1 cup white sugar
2 cups water	4 eggs
6 cups whole milk	1 teaspoon vanilla

Soak the tapioca in the water in the refrigerator for 24 hours, then drain off the water and add milk and salt. Bring to a boil. Slowly add the sugar. Reduce to a low heat, and let simmer for 5 minutes.

Separate the eggs, beating the yolks in one large bowl and the whites in another large bowl.

Very gradually add the hot tapioca mixture to the egg yolks, stirring carefully so as not to cook the eggs. Return the mixture to a saucepan, and bring to a boil, stirring constantly. Reduce heat and cook for 3 minutes. Remove from heat and add the hot mixture slowly to the beaten egg whites. Add the vanilla. Serve warm or chilled. Garnish with whipped cream or fruit.

An interesting variation is the addition of 1 cup of chocolate chips, folded in while the pudding is still warm.

FLAN

Julia claims that this recipe from her sister Tita is as easy as a dessert can be. She makes it look that way. Earlier flan recipes I tried were not nearly so easy.

SERVES 8

¼ cup water	one 14-ounce can of condensed milk
½ cup white sugar	
1 tablespoon butter	one 12-ounce can of evaporated milk
4 eggs	
2 egg yolks	1 to 2 teaspoons vanilla extract

Caramelize the sugar and water in a heavy-bottomed stainless-steel pan. To "caramelize," bring the mixture to a boil, and continue to boil until brown in color and quite thick. Handle carefully, because this liquid is hotter than hot.

THE NEW FAMILY COOKBOOK

Carefully pour the liquid caramel into the bottom of a soufflé dish, and allow to cool. Butter the sides of the dish.

In a separate bowl, mix the eggs, yolks, condensed and evaporated milk, and vanilla. Pour this mixture into the soufflé dish on top of the caramel. Place the soufflé dish in a larger pan containing ¼ inch of water. Cook in the oven at 325 degrees F for about 1 hour, or until a skewer inserted into the center comes out clean.

RASPBERRY SHERBET

This recipe originated with Sara and Berit's mother, Sonja Olson. It is probably the most elegant of simple recipes that I can imagine.

SERVES 6

    3 cups raspberry purée
    2 cups white sugar
    juice of 1 lemon (about 3 tablespoons)

Make a purée by running raspberries through a food mill to crush and remove most of the seeds. Combine this with the sugar and lemon juice. Beat the mixture until the sugar is dissolved. Place in a bowl in the freezer compartment, and stir every 20 minutes until well frozen.

RASPBERRY JAM

This simple jam is great for Christmas gifts.

YIELDS 2 PINTS

    4 cups raspberries
    3 cups sugar

Combine the raspberries and sugar in a heavy saucepan. Simmer. Stir frequently until jelled, about 10 to 15 minutes. Pour hot into hot jars and seal with canning lids and rings or melted paraffin.

RASPBERRY SAUCE

If you have the luxury of fresh raspberries, this makes an excellent sauce for cakes or ice cream. Of course, you could do it using frozen raspberries as well.

2 cups raspberries	3 tablespoons rum (optional)
2 tablespoons water	1 tablespoon cornstarch
½ cup white sugar	1 tablespoon water
juice of 1½ lemons (about 4 tablespoons)	

Cook the raspberries with the water, sugar, lemon juice, and rum until soft. If needed, thicken a bit with a mixture of equal parts cornstarch and water. Use caution: Add only a little at a time. Cool and purée.

BROWN SUGAR WHIPPED CREAM

Adding the rum gives this whipped cream an old Caribbean/New England connection, perfect for Cranberry Gingerbread (see recipe, page 112).

1 cup whipping cream, chilled	⅓ cup brown sugar
⅓ cup yogurt or sour cream, chilled	1½ teaspoons vanilla extract
	1½ teaspoons dark rum

Whip the cream with a power mixer until soft peaks form. Just before it is finished, add the yogurt, sugar, vanilla, and rum.

Note: You may prepare the cream 4 hours in advance and refrigerate.

GINGER WHIPPED CREAM

We liked the extra flavors in this whipped cream so much that we use it for lots of desserts, including Pumpkin Pecan Spice Cake (see recipe, page 111).

YIELDS 12 SERVINGS

1	cup whipping cream, chilled	1½	tablespoons dark rum
¼	cup sour cream or yogurt	¼	teaspoon ground ginger
2	tablespoons sugar		

Beat the cream until peaks begin to form, then add the yogurt, sugar, rum, and ginger. Beat until almost stiff.

You may prepare the whipped cream up to 5 hours ahead and refrigerate.

CHAPTER ELEVEN

SPECIAL EVENTS AND MENUS

T'S HARD TO SAY WHY I've chosen the particular group of items for this chapter. I guess it's a selection of food-related highlights that have punctuated my life. As I review the collection, I see evidence of the changes I have experienced over a couple of decades. It was nearly twenty years ago when I felt the apprehension about fixing a Thanksgiving dinner on my own for the first time. Now, for the past few years, my daughters have been assembling a group of non-holiday-travelers for a homemade-in-New-York-City-apartment turkey feast including stuffing and kale soup from this book. It seems my favorite holiday meal has become an important one for my daughters too.

Ethnic recipe groups are a result of travel adventures or the decision to try a new food style that is suddenly appealing. That appeal may come from sampling new flavors or from reading new evidence of the health benefits of a certain cuisine. I'm currently experimenting and practicing to develop a menu for a Japanese dinner. This quest began with the discovery of soba noodles and a desire to make soybeans part of our diet.

A SOUTH INDIAN DINNER

I've always had a special love for Indian food. After a month working in Mannipal (in the southern state of Karnataka), sampling all the vegetarian foods, and inquiring in many kitchens, I was able to put together a menu for a whole meal. If you include rice (see recipe, page 60), these recipes will serve 8 people.

♥♥♥ CHANNA (INDIAN-STYLE CHICK PEAS)

Soon after I started my vegetarian sojourn in India, I fell in love with this frequent appearance on the tali *(daily lunch plate). I finally secured a recipe from an obstetrician from Washington, D.C., who was visiting the medical school in Mannipal. Asafetida and mango powder are Indian spices that may require a trip to a natural food store.*

SERVES 8

¾ pound chick peas	1 teaspoon ground cumin
⅓ cup peanut oil	1½ teaspoons mango powder
1 pinch asafetida	½ teaspoon salt
½ teaspoon whole cumin seeds	juice of 1 lemon (about 2 to 3
½ teaspoon ground turmeric	tablespoons)
½ teaspoon chili powder	1 tablespoon cilantro leaves,
1 teaspoon ground coriander	chopped
seed	1 green chili, chopped

Sort, wash, soak, and cook the chick peas by bringing to a boil, and then simmering for 40 to 60 minutes, until tender. Drain, but save the cooking water.

Heat the oil in a large skillet. Add a pinch of asafetida and the whole cumin seeds. Sizzle for a few seconds. Add the turmeric, chili powder, coriander, cumin, mango powder, and salt. Then add the chick peas, and stir-fry for 3 to 4 minutes to mix the flavors. Finally, add the chick pea broth as needed to adjust the consistency (I prefer mine thick, not soupy), along with lemon juice, cilantro, and green chili.

♥ DAL

Sara requested the recipe for this exquisite dish from our one fancy meal of the Indian trip, namely at the Taj Mahal hotel in Bombay. If you can't find the authentic Indian Urad Dal, regular green-tan lentils will work fine.

SERVES 8

- 1 kilo (2.2 pounds) black Urad Dal
- 150 grams (about 5 ounces) red kidney beans
- 1 medium onion, sliced
- 5 tablespoons butter, divided
- chili powder, to taste
- 1 teaspoon black cardamom
- 1 teaspoon green cardamom
- 2 teaspoons fresh gingerroot, chopped
- 2 garlic cloves, chopped
- ½ to 1 cup Marinara Sauce (see recipe, page 94)
- ½ to 1 cup cream
- salt, to taste

In a large pot, cover the lentils with twice their depth of water. Bring to a boil and simmer, covered, for 20 to 30 minutes, until tender. Stir occasionally, and add water if necessary.

Given the small quantity of kidney beans, you may wish to use the canned variety. If you use dried beans, soak them overnight. In the morning, drain and cover with fresh water, and cook 40 to 60 minutes, until tender.

Sauté the onion in a little butter, stirring so it doesn't burn. Cook beyond the tender translucent stage, until the onions become brown in color.

Sauté the spices together, then add the lentils and kidney beans with 4 tablespoons butter and the marinara. Cook briefly. Add cream, salt to taste, and top with browned onions.

Note: This is Indian cooking. Vary the amounts of spices, ginger, and garlic according to your taste.

♥♥ INDIAN EGGPLANT WITH YOGURT SAUCE

This makes a nice vegetable addition to an Indian menu.

SERVES 8

2 medium or large eggplants, sliced
2 tablespoons ground coriander seeds
1½ teaspoons ground turmeric
8 cloves garlic, mashed
2 to 4 tablespoons water, divided
salt, to taste
⅓ to ½ cup olive oil

2 medium onions, sliced
2 to 3 zucchini, sliced
1 green bell pepper, cut into small strips
1 red bell pepper, cut into small strips
1½ to 2 cups yogurt

Salt the cut sides of the eggplant, and press to dehydrate.

Mix the coriander seeds, turmeric, garlic, 1 to 2 tablespoons water, and salt. Set aside.

In olive oil, one vegetable at a time, stir-fry the onions, eggplant, zucchini, and red and green bell peppers, spreading the fried vegetables on paper towels as each is finished.

Stir-fry the spice and garlic mixture for 2 minutes to dry the paste and fry the garlic. Add 1 to 2 tablespoons water. Stir once and turn off the heat. Add the yogurt and vegetables, and reheat to serving temperature. Or you may let the dish cool and serve at room temperature.

♥♥ RAITA

This chilled yogurt recipe is eaten as a means of cooling off the mouth when eating spicy South Indian dishes.

SERVES 8

1½ cups low-fat yogurt
2 tablespoons cilantro, chopped
½ cucumber, finely diced

¼ teaspoon chili powder
½ teaspoon ground cumin
½ teaspoon salt

Whisk the yogurt in a bowl until smooth. Add the cilantro, cucumber, chili powder, cumin, and salt. Stir well. Chill until ready to serve.

A SOUTH ASIAN FEAST

I don't know whether I was more inspired by my daughter Sara's Christmas gift of the South Asian cookbook, or by watching her prepare spring rolls. Sometime after enjoying the South Asian meal that she and Tom prepared for us, I put together the following combination for a South Asian menu that we've enjoyed many times.

♥♥ CHICKEN SATAY

SERVES 6

FOR THE MARINADE:

¼ cup fish sauce
juice of 1 lemon (about 2 to 3 tablespoons)

2 to 3 cloves garlic, crushed
salt and black pepper, to taste

FOR THE SAUCE:

1¼ cups light coconut milk
¾ cup smooth peanut butter
3 tablespoons fish sauce
1 tablespoon soy sauce

3 tablespoons fresh gingerroot, minced
3 tablespoons brown sugar
½ teaspoon ground red pepper

ADDITIONAL INGREDIENTS:

2 pounds chicken breast, sliced to a thickness of ½ inch or less
6 to 8 ounces snap pea or sunflower sprouts

2 to 3 carrots, grated
a handful of rice-stick noodles
⅓ cup peanut oil

Mix all the marinade ingredients, and marinate the sliced chicken breast for 6 to 10 hours in the refrigerator.

Prepare the satay sauce by combining the ingredients in a food processor with a metal blade.

Cook the rice-stick noodles in boiling water for 40 to 50 seconds, and rinse immediately in cold water to stop the cooking.

Prepare a serving platter with a layer of sprouts sprinkled with the grated carrots, then covered with the cooked rice-stick noodles.

Grill the chicken, preferably over a wood fire, cut into strips, and add to the platter with the sprouts and noodles. Lacking a wood fire, cut the chicken into strips and stir fry in peanut oil. Serve hot with satay sauce on the side for dipping.

♥♥♥ MUSHROOM VEGETABLE STIR-FRY WITH SOBA NOODLES

This is a great basic stir-fry recipe that you can play with. Try substituting other vegetables that you like. Add some cashews if you like them. Also consider using rice instead of the soba noodles.

SERVES 6

8 or more dried porcini mushrooms

2 cups hot water

4 cloves garlic, crushed

2 tablespoons fresh gingerroot, minced

3 to 4 carrots, peeled and grated

3 to 4 leeks, cut into thin strips 1½ inches long

1 bunch spinach, chopped coarsely

2½ teaspoons toasted sesame oil, divided

2 teaspoons cornstarch

3 teaspoons soy sauce

2 Portabello mushrooms, the tops sliced (discard the stems)

8 shitake mushrooms, cleaned and sliced

3 to 4 tablespoons peanut oil or canola oil

⅓ cup sake or dry vermouth

¾ pound soba noodles

Soften the porcini mushrooms in the hot water. Drain the mushrooms, preserving the water for later use. Then add the garlic and gingerroot to the mushrooms.

Cut up the vegetables as indicated.

Make a mushroom sauce by combining the reserved mushroom liquid with enough water to regain the original 2-cup volume. Add 1½ teaspoons of the sesame oil, cornstarch, and soy sauce. Whisk to mix thoroughly.

Heat the peanut or canola oil in a wok. Add the softened, dried mushroom mixture. Stir-fry for 1 minute. Add the carrots and leeks. Stir-fry for an additional 1 to 2 minutes. Add the sake or vermouth and the fresh mushrooms and spinach. Cook for another minute. Finally, add the mushroom sauce, and cook, stirring, until the sauce thickens slightly.

Cook the soba noodles for 4 to 4½ minutes. Rinse immediately in cold water, and toss with 1 teaspoon of sesame oil. Remove the mushroom stir-fry from the wok. Mix with the soba noodles and serve.

THANKSGIVING TURKEY AND ALL THE FIXINGS

Presenting a Thanksgiving spread for friends and relatives can be a daunting task the first few years that you're on you own in the kitchen. I hope that the following information helps by putting all the standard things together with a time schedule and all the details that I've found work well for me. The beauty of this arrangement when you're about to embark on a Thanksgiving dinner for a large gathering is that most of the work can be done the night before so that you can be relaxed on Thanksgiving day.

When choosing your turkey, plan on 1 pound per person. This is generous, but allows for hearty appetites and some leftovers.

Of course, we're biased toward fresh Vermont turkeys, but they're not available everywhere. Ask about fresh turkeys in a natural food co-op or specialized food market. Lacking a reliable source for fresh, a frozen turkey from the supermarket is perfectly acceptable.

I've not said more about "other menu ideas," purposely leaving these somewhat to individual creativity. For example, our sweet potatoes are baked in halves with a brown-sugar butter sauce if my mother brings them; but are baked in halves with only a little olive oil, salt, and black pepper if *we* make them.

SCHEDULE

Three days before Thanksgiving:

1. If you choose a frozen turkey, start thawing it in the refrigerator.

The day before Thanksgiving:

1. If you find a fresh turkey, this is the time to get it into your refrigerator.
2. Prepare turkey (see page 130).
3. Begin making stuffing (see recipe, page 132).
4. Consider other menu items that you might want to prepare, depending on your time frame for the next day.

Thanksgiving Day:

1. Finish preparing stuffing.

2. Begin roasting the turkey and stuffing 2 to 3 hours before you plan to eat.
3. If you haven't made a roux for gravy, do so now.
4. Cook potatoes to be mashed shortly before serving, saving the water you cook them in to use in the gravy.
5. While the turkey is "resting" out of the oven, mash potatoes and finish gravy.
6. Hope that other menu items were completed prior to the final

TURKEY PREPARATION

The beauty of this method is that the breast and legs will both cook for the proper amount of time rather than allowing the legs to become too dry from overcooking. You'll find that the thighs slice beautifully like slicing a sausage. Since your turkey has been disassembled, it no longer has a cavity in which to place the stuffing. That's not a problem, as stuffing tastes better baked in a dish, and you can make a lot more than you would be able to stuff into a turkey.

The "real" start is a visit to the turkey farm to pick up your fresh Vermont turkey. Then the night before Thanksgiving, disassemble the turkey by removing the wing ends, the leg and thigh from each side, and the entire back. Bone the thigh (it's really impossible to remove the drumstick bone), and tie the thigh meat back together with string. Cut the bones, neck, back, and wing ends into 1- to 2-inch pieces to make stock for gravy and stuffing.

ROASTING THE TURKEY

YIELDS ABOUT 1 POUND PER PERSON

1   turkey (1 pound per person)
Stuffing (see recipe, page 132)
3   tablespoons olive oil
6   carrots, cut into quarters, then
    4 inches long

2   onions, quartered
8   stalks celery, cut into 4-inch
    pieces

Preheat the oven to 450 degrees F.
   Place the stuffing on a large, round sheet in the center of a roasting rack. Surround the stuffing with an aluminum fence. If you find a large disposable aluminum baking dish, that will work even better. Place the breast over the stuffing with the wings tied. Brush with olive oil, and cover with cheesecloth. Place it in the oven, and immediately bring the temperature down to 325 degrees F. Baste every 30 minutes. It will take about 2 hours to roast a 12 pound turkey, and 2½ to 3 hours for a 15 to 18 pound turkey.

Place the leg/thigh pieces onto the baking rack about 1½ hours before the breast will be finished. During the last hour of baking, add pieces of carrots, onions, and celery to flavor the juice. There should be a cup of juice in the pan under the rack when the turkey is done. Test for doneness with a meat thermometer. Temperature for the breast should be 170 degrees F, for the thigh, 180 degrees F.

Remove the meat to a platter for 30 minutes before carving.

BROWN TURKEY STOCK

Going to the extra effort to prepare this turkey stock will make the cooks in your gathering sit up and take notice of your culinary abilities.

YIELDS ABOUT 2 QUARTS OF STOCK

	turkey bones, neck, back, and wing-ends, cut into 1- to 2-inch pieces	4 to 6	cups chicken or vegetable stock
¼	cup peanut oil	2	stalks celery with leaves
1½	cups carrots, chopped	1	bay leaf
1½	cups onions, chopped		several sprigs thyme
¾	cup dry vermouth		salt and black pepper, to taste

Brown the turkey pieces in the peanut oil in a large skillet (cover to prevent splattering). Halfway through the browning process, add the carrots and onions. Transfer the mixture to a heavy saucepan, and deglaze the skillet with the vermouth. Then add the chicken or vegetable stock, celery, bay leaf, thyme, salt, and black pepper. Strain and chill. Use the stock for gravy or stuffing.

STUFFING

It's a good idea to begin making the stuffing the night before, so that some of the flavors can be mixing during the night.

SERVES 12 TO 14, WITH SOME LEFTOVERS

2	medium onions, chopped	⅓	cup pine nuts
1	tablespoon butter	½	cup dried currants
½	turkey liver, chopped	2	eggs, beaten
1 to 2	cups turkey stock (see recipe, page 129)		grated nutmeg, to taste
			salt and black pepper, to taste
2	loaves day-old bread, cubed with crusts removed	¼	cup fresh basil, chopped
		1	tablespoon fresh sage, chopped
⅓	cup parsley, chopped		
4 to 5	stalks celery, sliced	1	tablespoon capers
2	apples, cored and sliced		

OPTIONAL:
1 to 1½ cups mushrooms, sliced and sautéed

Sauté the onions in butter. Add the chopped liver and some turkey stock. Mix this with all the remaining ingredients, adding turkey stock as necessary to moisten the mixture. Remember, it should only be moist, not soupy. Store in the refrigerator overnight to mix the flavors.

Bake the stuffing with the turkey on Thanksgiving Day.

GRAVY

Be sure to make plenty to go with the leftover mashed potatoes and stuffing.

YIELDS 6 CUPS

7 to 8	tablespoons turkey fat, skimmed from the top of the chilled stock	1	cup potato water (water used to cook potatoes) or dry vermouth
½	cup flour		salt and black pepper, to taste
6	cups hot turkey stock (see recipe, page 131)		

While the turkey is roasting, or the night before, make a roux, the fat/flour base for the gravy. Blend the turkey fat and flour with a wooden spoon. Stir over moderate heat until the roux turns a walnut-brown color. Vigorously whisk in the hot turkey stock. Simmer, stirring, for 10 minutes. If prepared ahead, refrigerate until needed. When the turkey is done, complete the gravy by deglazing the pan with potato water or vermouth. Add the pan product to the gravy base. Reduce, over moderately high heat, and season with salt and pepper.

OTHER MENU IDEAS FOR THANKSGIVING

Leek and Carrot Sauté (see recipe, page 49)
Leeks and Sundried Tomatoes (see recipe, page 50)
Sweet potatoes
Mashed Potatoes (see recipe, page 44)
Sourdough French Bread (see recipe, page 68)
Mushroom and Wild Rice Soup (see recipe, page 38)
Tossed green salad
Cranberry Gingerbread (see recipe, page 112)
Pumpkin Pie (see recipe, page 104)

FOOD GENES

by Berit Eichner

It is a rare phone conversation between my father and me that doesn't eventually turn to what one of us has eaten, read about, cooked, or sampled. Recently I bragged about the Thanksgiving feast that my sister and I, our respective partners, and friends cooked in her Brooklyn apartment:

"Well, I made the pumpkin pie, and even though two other people made pumpkin, too, mine was the first to go!" I said.

"It must have been Grandma's famous pie crust. Did you use Crisco, or just butter?" Long pause. "Actually, it came from the freezer section in a Pillsbury container."

My father is patient, forgiving even. "Well, okaaay. What spices did you use? How long did you boil the pumpkin?"

A longer pause. "The stuff in the can already has spices in it."

Luckily it is not possible to see long eye rolls or someone making the sign of the cross over the phone. At this point, though, it's unnecessary. I know, after all, how I've damaged the family name already. I grew up without seeing a single name-brand item in our kitchen besides the occasional box of Rice Krispies or Grape-Nuts, and most meals evolved from garden to table. How then, could I be proud of canned pie mix dumped into a frozen shell?

So far, I have yet to see a recipe for how to balance the ingredients of a proud heritage of culinary expertise on both sides of the family with an equally flavorful twenty-something New York City lifestyle. Like oil and water, they seem resistant to mixing. After all, among friends I *am* considered a cook because I have a refrigerator with more food in it than just olives and souring milk. I occasionally have friends over for meals that don't just involve the dumping of white cartons from the Vietnamese place downstairs. This, however, is a far cry from making one's own sundried tomatoes, as my father subtly reminds me.

Even when my boyfriend and I sit down to our regular dinners, I get pangs of guilt as I pour (sorry, it's the truth) marinara from a jar, or when the first thing in my grocery basket every week is a plastic tub of hummus. (I know, I know, it's so much cheaper and tastier to make from scratch, and so simple . . .)

And then, just when I figure I will be the processed-foods queen, or black sheep of the family, I realize that I've got more of these foodie genes in me than I care to admit. Even if I don't crank out quart tubs of hummus, and the occasional bag of McDonald's French fries still finds its way into my hands, I can't boil out every bit of "cook" flavor in me. In fact, it seems to have been reduced to a thick, rich broth somewhere in my veins. The effects of growing up in a family that loved food, from its origins in the earth to the dinner table, have lingered.

I haven't missed eating a decent breakfast in years. Dinner is not dinner unless a table is set and at least a few food groups are represented. Plus, I love food in all its forms. Growing up eating everything from scrapple to puréed leeks has me taking advantage of every empanada, sushi, and lentil dish New York has to offer.

My food genes have also taught me that "simple is better." After a series of small dinner parties for which my boyfriend and I painstakingly recreated dishes from *Cooks* magazine, leaving us both bitter and exhausted, we learned to reduce meal anxiety. We actually looked forward to guests' arrival by making simpler dishes, such as my father's kale soup, my mother's puttanesca sauce, and linguini. We were able to smile when they rang our doorbell, and they even smiled back as they ate our food. I don't even think anyone faked it, either.

So, here I've got my bulk-size bag of New York resistance to cooking for oneself, along with a potent stock of excellent cooks in my family. What do I do? Do I keep hiding the Doritos bags and instant coffee when my parents visit? Or, do I stop my quest to try every ethnic restaurant in New York and learn how to cook it myself? I think there is a balance there somewhere. Luckily, in the meantime, my father seems willing to wait it out. He passes on recipes, feeds me delicious homemade meals on my visits home, and makes a reservation at a sumptuous restaurant whenever visiting us in New York. Plus, I know someday he's going to try that pumpkin pie of mine (or Pillsbury's) and love it.

CHAPTER TWELVE

COMMUNION

AND FINALLY, BERIT AND SARA, when you have memorized all the recipes in this manual and accumulated a dozen more fine cookbooks, have acquired a KitchenAid mixer for making bread, and a Cuisinart to aid you in all that chopping, have found the source for the best fresh produce, and have refined your techniques for pie crust and raspberry sherbet—remember that the ultimate goal is the pleasure of communion, the spiritual feast that can be part of eating with those you love. In the coming together of any two or more of us to partake of the bread and the cup—whether it's as lavish as the banquet that Babette prepared for her mistress, or just a cup of coffee shared between two lovers waking in the morning—it is the togetherness of partaking and the love that goes into the preparation and planning that finally makes food such an important part of our lives. We need it to nourish our bodies, but without love and sharing, food becomes mere fodder—no different than that simple fuel that was used to recharge the teams of horses in those old Nebraska days.

I remember, in 1975, your communion around Abu Ali's giant stone oven in the old city of Jerusalem. You helped him prepare your version of Arab pizza. I remember you offering some to the old Palestinian woman who came in off the streets. Yes, she probably was Muslim, but her beseeching eyes and outstretched hands could have been those of any supplicant at any altar to receive the Eucharist. Thank you for learning the Arab style of sharing food: *tfaddel,* or "come eat this bread with me."

In 1980, in Cornwall, the three of us had our private communion every morning, sharing the hot breakfast I had prepared at the wood stove. It was different every day. French toast, coarse-floured pancakes, hot five-grain cereal (or was it seven?). Sometimes you thought this stuff was too healthy. But it was a chance to be together, preparing ourselves for the day before you got on the school bus.

In 1985, it was a different world for all of us. The family was at odds. We had a new communion ritual: all pitching in to prepare a meal efficiently after school and work. A chance to talk over our pains and occasional joys while sharing the food that we had prepared together. For those moments at the table, we could sit facing each other and talk with no distractions. It's funny that food is not a distraction in an around-the-table conversation. I think it's because we share not only the taste, but also, at times, the idea of the bounties of nature, and a reminder of the effort and love that goes into the planning and final preparation of what we put in our mouths.

These days, our coming together happens less frequently because you're on your own. Our new family continues to evolve, but we still treasure the time around the table. I've come to realize that what I want to pass on to you are memories, and of course, advice about those things, those foods, that we've all learned to enjoy together. I'm reminded of hearing about a strange new cookbook just released. A group of women, facing their final days in a Nazi concentration camp, collected their memories of their favorite meals from better days, when the families were together. One woman wrote these on scraps of paper. Miraculously, they reached her surviving daughter just this last year.

May you be blessed always, not only by the rich tastes, but also by the love and communion that comes with preparing and sharing nourishing food.

A GOOD CUP OF COFFEE

"**S**O COFFEE IS A HEALTHY FOOD?" I hear you ask. No. Coffee isn't even a food, but when it is good, it is a seductive bouquet and a mouthful of rich, complex favors. And it is a drug that helps most of us get a start on our day. It's a commodity second in economic importance only to petroleum in the United States. As a crop, coffee has long been a political tool for oppression and colonialism around the world. (Read all about coffee in *Uncommon Grounds,* by Mark Pendergrast, published by Basic Books.)

I grew up with a "bad cup of coffee" in Nebraska. Our coffee was brewed from inferior beans, a brownish liquid so thin as to be sour and transparent. No doubt the custom of weak coffee was born out of the frugal nature of Central Plains farmers. But for special events, they made an almost good cup of coffee by doubling the concentration and by mixing an egg with the ground coffee, stirring it into a large pot of water just as the boiling point was reached. Then they immediately turned off the heat, added the crushed egg shell, and, after a minute or two for brewing, drizzled in a cup of cold water to settle everything. Do that, and you will have an absolutely clear cup of coffee.

In contrast to my own family in the 1950s, our poor and frugal Dominican farmer friends would never skimp on the "strength" of their coffee. They simply drink a smaller cup. I'm on their side. I'll take two ounces of the real thing over a potful of bad coffee any day.

Until this chapter, I've tried in this book to tell you how to use food to make healthy changes in your eating style, so that you'll be around to cook for your grandchildren and teach them how to eat healthfully. But I want to use coffee, a non-food, and a luxury beverage with no nutritional value, as a tool to talk about another kind of healthy change. I want to shift the focus from personal health to a look at the source of coffee, the hillsides where it grows, the soil, the insects, and birds, rainfall, and other plants that make up the total ambiance, the ecosystem of those hills. I want to consider the farmers who work so hard to nurture the coffee trees and handle the fruit of those trees in a manner that will ensure that quality is preserved until it reaches your cup.

So here is the story of our adventure into the world of coffee. I hope when you buy your next bag of beans you'll consider not only the flavor, but also think about being friendly enough to the coffee farms so they'll still be producing for generations to come. Consider fair trade issues, so that farm workers can be healthy too, so that their children can have a better life in the coffee-growing industry.

CAFÉ ALTA GRACIA—A SUSTAINABLE COFFEE

We came up with the name "Alta Gracia" when we purchased our land. The name and the picture on our label refer to a legendary Dominican religious figure, Altagracia. The words that make up her name mean "high grace." This symbolizes for us our *finca* in the central Dominican mountains and our purpose there.

Lofty terminology, you say? Well, we have to aim high and work hard to turn around two major injustices in our little corner of the coffee-producing world. First, coffee is an industry based on poverty, the poverty of small owners and workers in the countries of origin. Second, major destruction of the forest canopy in the coffee growing lands has occurred during the last twenty-five years. This shade cover in coffee farms is a habitat comparable to traditional rain forest—a bit tamer perhaps, but just as important for migratory birds and other wildlife, for the health of the soil under it, and for retention of the rain that falls upon that soil.

It was a writing job of Julia's that led us to Los Dajaos, a community of forty-three families that we had previously only driven past. Naty, José, and Fredy told us about their community project/cooperative, Asociación Agricultores Los Dajaos (ASADA), a grassroots organization committed to the practice and teaching of organic farming, and to improving standards of hygiene, health, and education in the community. We decided within twenty-four hours that this might be the spot for us to finally settle into for a project that might benefit our other homeland.

By the fall of 1997, we had purchased approximately 60 acres of essentially bare land at an elevation of 1,200 to 1,400 meters. We found about 5 acres of old abandoned coffee plants running through the center of the property, all shaded by guama trees. Our first project was to get these cleaned up and pruned and fed in hopes that we would have a small crop of coffee to pick the following January. It was fortunate that we heard from Mr. Brian Rudert at the United States Agency for International Development (U.S. AID) mission to the Dominican Republic. He was working with members of our Los Dajaos community to help them convert their coffee production to a bird-safe organic coffee. This was a major project, because it meant the conversion of shadeless coffee plots to shaded plots, and a complete elimination of chemical pesticides. It was the beginning of our own awareness of the importance of shade-grown coffee. Brian Rudert told us about research by Joe Wunderlich in the Los Dajaos area in the early 1990s that showed that coffee grown under diverse species of shade trees had large migratory bird populations compared to the meager showing of birds in the shadeless coffee fields.

Once the idea was planted in our minds, we found other examples that shade-grown coffee is a way to protect migratory songbirds, including the Bicknell's Thrush that summers in the highlands of Vermont. The Audubon Society, the Smithsonian Institution Migratory Bird Center, and the Vermont Institute of National Science are all trying to promote the purchase of shade-grown coffee as a means of conserving habitats of migratory songbirds.

Since our "old coffee" was already fully shaded, and because we knew that reforestation of our farm was one of our prime goals, it was only natural that we should commit ourselves to planting and growing and producing 100 percent shade-grown coffee. We were already committed to 100 percent organic farming.

Ironically, growing coffee under shade is not a new "green" fad. Traditionally, coffee has been grown under shade from the time this plant was first introduced into this hemisphere in the early 1700s.

But, as with the rest of agriculture, the coffee-growing industry has had to endure a period of "technification." This involved development of a dwarf variety of coffee planted much more densely and without shade trees of any kind, enabling from two to three times the usual production of coffee. To be "successful," this shadeless method requires heavy doses of pesticides and chemical fertilizers. During the 1970s and 1980s, a large portion of Latin American coffee farms were stripped of the shade trees that had shielded the heirloom coffee plants from sun and had also provided cover for migratory songbirds. Wiping out the insect population with pesticides only added further insult to the old system, and the songbirds started to disappear. Fortunately, some of the poorest farmers on the smallest plots of land could not afford pesticides or chemical fertilizers and therefore could not afford to convert their farms to the shadeless varieties of coffee. By the early 1990s researchers and birders began to notice the huge difference in bird populations (both numbers of birds and numbers of species) on the small forested farms as compared to the large shadeless plantations.

And not only the birds are at stake with the shift to "technified" coffee. Small farmers and coffee farmworkers are some of the lowest-paid laborers in the world. Now in many instances they are also being subjected to chronic poisoning by use of pesticides. Their lives are also changed as they have moved away from growing the diverse shade species that included timber production, citrus fruits, avocados, nut trees, and other income producers. It's difficult for small farmers to be dependent on a single product in today's market.

About the time we started our project, we realized that we faced a big challenge. Despite growing up on an organic farm in Nebraska, followed by a couple of decades of organic gardening in Vermont, I had a lot to learn in order to raise organic coffee in the Dominican Republic. Furthermore, to follow our conscience, we needed to be aware of the plight of the poor workers who were going to be producing the crops for us. In the past few years, we have embarked on an attempt to learn all we can about tropical organic agriculture, about what makes up diverse shade cover, and about the intricacies of the coffee market, so that we can build a model farm with all the ancillary aspects that will provide a healthy environment for workers and their families, both on our own farm and in the larger community. We formed the Altagracia Foundation, a nonprofit organization that will produce coffee and other agricultural products, in order to provide for the social and economic well-being and health of the workers. Eventually, we plan to build an educational center for promoting literacy, the arts, and education about sustainable agriculture for the broader community around Los Dajaos.

We are continuing to harvest high-quality coffee from our rejuvenated old plants, and have also had a first picking from some of the early plantings of our own. After de-pulping, our beans are washed, then sundried, and finally hand-sorted to ensure the best quality in the cup. We continue to plant, now only heirloom varieties (*tipica* and *borbon*). In order to ensure a steady supply of these varieties, we are raising our own plants in a nursery on our property. Before the coffee plants are set into the field, the soil is prepared and a groundcover (red clover of the Vermont variety) and rows of shade trees are planted. We are using two levels of shade. The tall species include aguacatilla, cedro, almendra, and grevilea. In addition to a high-shade canopy, these will produce small fruits for birds and valuable high-quality wood from those trees that are eventually thinned out of the row. A second level of shade includes various species of citrus, trees pruned for use as firewood, macadamia nuts, cashews, and avocados. From these trees, along with the vegetable gardens also being prepared on the farm, most of the foods consumed by the farmworkers will come from the farm itself.

We have also managed to build substantial housing for the caretakers and their families, to provide a stable supply of clean water, and to install solar panels. Electric lights are needed for the literacy program. For a few hours in the evening, everyone involved in the project is attempting to learn basic reading and writing.

By now, we have need for helping hands in the education process. In January 2000, a first group of students from Middlebury College went to Los Dajaos for a course called "Writing in the Wilds." Half of their course time was spent in agricultural and literacy projects in the community. The students and everyone in the community who was involved in the course gave it high marks. Seeing this enthusiasm, like tasting a cup of Café Altagracia, is a sweet reward for all the efforts we all have invested. Finally, I believe our dream is a process underway.

INDEX

CHELSEA GREEN

Sustainable living has many facets. Chelsea Green's celebration of the sustainable arts has led us to publish trend-setting books about organic gardening, solar electricity and renewable energy, innovative building techniques, regenerative forestry, local and bioregional democracy, and whole foods. The company's published works, while intensely practical, are also entertaining and inspirational, demonstrating that an ecological approach to life is consistent with producing beautiful, eloquent, and useful books, videos, and audio cassettes.

For more information about Chelsea Green, or to request a free catalog, call toll-free (800) 639-4099, or write to us at P.O. Box 428, White River Junction, Vermont 05001. Visit our Web site at www.chelseagreen.com.

Chelsea Green's titles include:

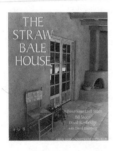 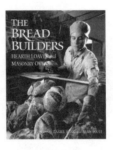 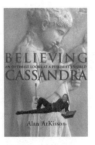

The Straw Bale House
The New Independent Home
The Natural House
Serious Straw Bale
The Beauty of
    Straw Bale Homes
The Resourceful Renovator
Independent Builder
The Rammed Earth House
The Passive Solar House
The Earth-Sheltered House
Wind Energy Basics
The Solar Living Sourcebook
A Shelter Sketchbook
Mortgage-Free!
Hammer. Nail. Wood.
Toil: Building Yourself

The Bread Builders
The Co-op Cookbook
Whole Foods Companion
Simple Food for the
    Good Life
The Apple Grower
The Flower Farmer
Forest Gardening
Passport to Gardening
The New Organic Grower
Breed Your Own
    Vegetable Varieties
Four-Season Harvest
Solar Gardening
Straight-Ahead Organic
The Contrary Farmer
Good Spirits

Believing Cassandra
Gaviotas: A Village to
    Reinvent the World
Loving and Leaving the
    Good Life
Scott Nearing: The Making
    of a Homesteader
Who Owns the Sun?
Global Spin:
    The Corporate Assault
on Environmentalism
Hemp Horizons
Beyond the Limits
The Man Who Planted Trees
The Northern Forest
Seeing Nature
Stone Circles